ONE FOR THE RECORD

By George Plimpton

THE RABBIT'S UMBRELLA (juvenile)

OUT OF MY LEAGUE

WRITERS AT WORK, VOLUMES I-IV (editor)

PAPER LION

THE BOGEY MAN

THE AMERICAN LITERARY ANTHOLOGY, VOLUMES I-III (editor)

AMERICAN JOURNEY: THE TIMES OF ROBERT F. KENNEDY
   (with Jean Stein)

MAD DUCKS AND BEARS

ONE FOR THE RECORD

ONE
FOR THE RECORD

The inside story of Hank Aaron's
chase for the home-run record

GEORGE PLIMPTON

1817

HARPER & ROW, PUBLISHERS
New York, Evanston, San Francisco, London

ISBN: 0-06-013373-2

LIBRARY OF CONGRESS CATALOG CARD NUMBER: 74-7026

For T.H.G.

Acknowledgments

The author wishes to acknowledge the help and support of a number of people: Pat Ryan of *Sports Illustrated*, who originally assigned the story of Hank Aaron's chase and overtaking of Babe Ruth's record which has been considerably expanded in what follows; and Jim Kaplan of the same magazine, whose research and advice have been of great benefit; Roger Cooper of Bantam Books, who edited the pictorial section; the management of the Atlanta Braves, especially Dick Cecil, Donald Davidson, and Bob Hope; those who provided stories and insights (acknowledged in the book), particularly Ralph Branca, Jim Bouton, Jim Brosnan, Joe Garagiola, Henry Greenberg, and Tony Kubek; Molly McKaughan, whose abilities under difficult conditions were exemplary; and also, by no means least, the subject himself, for whom the author trusts this book will be a deserving tribute.

It was a simple act by an unassuming man which touched an enormous circle of people, indeed an entire country. It provided an instant which people would remember for decades—exactly what they were doing at the time of the home run that beat Babe Ruth's great record of 714 home runs which had stood for 39 years, whether they were watching it on a television set, or heard it over the car radio while driving along the turnpike at night, or whether a neighbor leaned over a picket fence and told them about it the next morning.

Its effect was far-reaching, and more powerful than one would expect from the act of hitting a ball over a fence. The Mexico sports correspondent from El Sol de Mexico, *almost overcome with emotion, ended his piece on the Aaron 715th home run with thanks to God. "We 'ived through this historic moment, the most fabulous in the world. Thanks to God we witnessed this moment of history."*

In Japan the huge headlines in Tokyo's premier sports daily read haikulike: WHITE BALL DANCES THROUGH ATLANTA'S WHITE MIST and under the subhead I SAW IT the correspondent began: "In my Atlanta hotel room I now begin writing this copy. I know I have to be calm. But I find it impossible to prevent my writing hand from continuing to shake . . ."

It caused tragedy. In Jacksonville, Florida, a taxicab driver shot himself when his wife pulled him out of his chair in front of the television to send him out to work just as he was settling down to the game. He died before the home run was hit.

In what might have seemed an illogical place, the instant caught the commissioner of baseball, Bowie Kuhn, addressing a Cleveland Indian Booster dinner in the Cleveland Stadium Club. In the controversy which had boiled up over Aaron's wish to skip the

1

Cincinnati series and open in Atlanta before his hometown fans, the commissioner had ruled against him and ordered him to play. Kuhn had vowed to be on hand for 715, but the moment found him on the dais reminiscing about Johnny Allen, the Indian's pitcher famed for disconcerting batters with a tattered sleeve on his pitching arm.

Almost everyone else in baseball was in front of a television set. In Kansas City the ancient black pitcher Satchel Paige had seventeen of his family crowded around ("all these sisters-in-law of mine") and when they saw the ball hit they began shouting and they could hear the people next door carrying on the same way.

For those who sat in the stadium in Atlanta their recollections would be especially intimate—the sharp cork-pop sound of the bat hitting the ball, startlingly audible in that split second of suspense before the crowd began a roar that lasted for more than ten minutes. Perhaps that is what they would remember— how people stood in front of their seats and sucked in air and bellowed it out in a sustained tribute that no other athlete has ever received. Or perhaps they would remember the wonder at how easy and inevitable it seemed—that having opened the season in Cincinnati by hitting the tying home run number 714 with his first swing of the year, it was obviously appropriate that the man called "Supe" by his teammates (for Superman) was going to duplicate the feat in Atlanta with his first swing of that game to break the record. That was why 53,775 had come. Or perhaps they would remember the odd way the stadium emptied after the excitement of the fourth inning, as if the crowd felt that what they had seen would be diluted by sitting through any more baseball that night.

But finally there were those few in the core of that immense circle—the participants themselves—who would be the ones most keenly touched: the pitcher, in this case a gap-toothed pleasant veteran named Al Downing who of the more than one hundred National League pitchers happened to be the one who threw a fast ball at a certain moment that did not tail away *properly; the hitter, Henry Aaron himself, for whom the event, despite his grace in dealing with it, had become so traumatic that little in the instant was to be relished except the relief that it had been done; the Braves' sports announcer, whose imagination for months had been working up words to describe the event to the outside world; and a young bullpen pitcher who would reach in the air and establish contact with a ball whose value as baseball's greatest talisman had been monetarily pegged at $25,000 and whose sentimental value was incalculable. . . .*

The Observer

It was about eleven o'clock on the Opening Day morning when we left for Riverfront Stadium—a writer friend and I walking over from the hotel. It's just a short walk from downtown Cincinnati. We bought some heated peanuts from an elderly vendor in top hat and tails and brown shoes. The wind was strong and he reached up and held his top hat in place while he filled the coarse paper bags. The tornadoes had come through the area the afternoon before, touching their funnels down within miles, but now the weather was clear, the wind snapping the baseball pennants stiff around the rim of the stadium.

"Is Billingham still scheduled to pitch?" I asked. "I don't know anything about him."

"A big baby-faced guy. He's good."

"How'd you like to be in his shoes?"

"You ever see Aaron hit a home run?" my friend asked.

"I saw him hit 713 on the second-to-last day of last season," I said. "I almost saw him hit 712. I was riding in a taxi from the Houston airport, just rushing to get to the Astrodome because I was writing the *Sports Illustrated* story on his chase of Ruth, really urging the driver on, 'Faster! Faster!' He was moving along about 80 miles an hour. Aaron came up, we could hear it on the car radio, in an early inning, and he hit one. I cried out in despair and slumped back in my seat. The driver looked around and said that, boy, was I *some* sort of fan . . ."

"Right on the job." The writer laughed.

"Well, I tried. When I got to the Astrodome, Bill Acree, who's the Braves' equipment manager, showed me the bat he hit it with . . . it was splintered *against*

5

the grain, which he'd never seen before. Unbelievable power. The ball had gone right between the hands of a guy reaching for it in left field and it hit an iron rail and bounced practically back in the infield."

We strolled along in the sun. We leaned on the balustrade, watching the traffic flow below on the highway.

"What's your angle on the story?" he asked.

"Well, my original idea was to deal with the artifacts themselves—like that splintered bat. Do you know Irwin Shaw's great war novel, *The Young Lions*? Well, his original notion was to take the bullet that killed his hero and take it back to its genesis, and write about all the people involved in turning a piece of iron ore in the ground into something that ends up in a soldier's body—the miners, the munition workers, the generals, the guy that wears the thing in his bandolier and shoves it into his rifle clip, and how these two—the bullet and the soldier—come together in some glade in the Ardennes. He discarded it finally— too artificial and cumbersome, I suppose . . ."

"I can guess," the writer said. "You want to do the same with the ball Aaron hits. You want to go back to the goddamn *cow*, for Chrissake, or the horse, whatever the ball is made of, right back to the animal grazing on some Andalusian meadow . . ."

"Something like that," I said lamely. "And, you know . . . who sewed the stitches, and who packages it in the red Spalding box, and the umpire who rubs it up and stamps it with a special number, and the pitcher, of course. There's an awful·lot of research, I agree . . ."

"Whew!"

"And the bat, of course—an ash tree."

"Oh Christ! And some guy coming along with an ax."

"The idea has upset you. I can tell."

"I keep thinking of that cow of yours—standing out there, and some kid coming along with a rope to lead the cow to the slaughterhouse, and that I'm going to have to *read* what you write about it."

"Well, I've dropped the whole idea. I couldn't have handled the cow business, I agree."

"What have you decided to do instead?" he asked after a while.

"I thought maybe I'd adapt the concept to the four principals involved in the home run—Henry Aaron, of course, the batter; the pitchers, whoever they are, maybe Billingham this afternoon will be one; and then the fans who catch the balls—715 I hear is now worth $25,000—all people who are obviously going to be affected by number 714 and 715 in the most decisive way."

"Who's the fourth?"

"A fellow called Milo Hamilton who is the broadcaster for the Atlanta Braves. He will be announcing the event to the outside world . . . he told me last fall that he was going to prepare a phrase . . . maybe something really terrific . . . to say when the ball sails over the fence."

"So that's what you're going to do?"

"Yes, I think so."

"Write about those four people."

"Yes."

"You promise to forget the cow?"

"Absolutely."

The Pitcher

The poor goon. All those years toiling on the mound, the area Early Wynn referred to as the "office" —peering down the long alley toward the plate at those constant disturbers of his sense of well-being settling into their stances and flicking their bats—to look down one day and find Henry *Aaron* there, standing easily in the farthest reaches of the batter's box looking out, the large, peaceful, dark face with the big eyes and the high forehead, and knowing that one mistake, one small lapse of concentration and ability would place his name forever in the record book as having thrown one of the "immortal gophers," either the one that tied, or more particularly the one breaking Ruth's record of 714.

For the last weeks of the 1973 season and now the first games of 1974 those pitchers scheduled in the rotation against the Braves have been involved in a sort of cosmic game of Russian roulette—it being inevitable that a pair of them, or perhaps even one, would be responsible for giving up the 714th and 715th home runs. It is a traumatic situation for them. In the left-field seats a forest of raised fishnets and gloved hands rises and sways in expectation. The pitcher is practically the only person in the park who does not want to see the home run hit. Even some of his own team-mates would not be displeased to see the last historic hits of Aaron's chase of Ruth's record, though they might be judicious enough to keep it to themselves. In the penultimate week of the 1973 season, I heard about a scuffle that had almost broken out in the Los Angeles dugout when a couple of the younger Dodgers, casting aside their team affiliation, began urging a long Aaron drive out of the park—"Get on over; get out!"— carried away in their hope to see a part of history; they got some hard stares and shoving from one or two of the more aggressively competitive of their elders, especially Andy Messersmith, who is not only a strong team man but a pitcher hardly agreeable to seeing one of his kind humbled.

On the last day of the 1973 season I remember getting a sense of how it affected a pitcher. Dave Roberts, the Houston Astros' right-hander, was scheduled to pitch against the Braves. Before the game, he sat in front of his locker looking crestfallen. He was awfully jittery. "You know what's going on in my mind?" he said to me. "What I should be doing is concentrating on my seventeenth victory of the year. But I've been thinking about *him*. I thought about him all last night. He was just deposited there in my mind. What really got me was that I knew that he wasn't thinking about me at *all*. I wished I'd known his home telephone number, so's I could have called him every twenty minutes. 'How's it going, Hank?'—just to let him know I was around."

It turned out that Roberts's hotel room was equipped with a cassette receiver on the TV set which allowed him to choose from a number of films provided by the management. Haphazardly, during the restless night, he made a selection and sat down on the edge of the bed to discover he was watching *The Poseidon Adventure,* the catastrophe-laden film about a cruise ship overturning in the Mediterranean. "Not the best therapy," he said. "It was so inappropriate considering what I faced the next day that I turned it off after a few minutes."

In that game Roberts survived three Aaron turns at bat by giving up three singles which raised the batter's average to .301; then, with his nervous system perhaps betraying him, the pitcher pulled a muscle in his back in the middle of the seventh inning and was removed. In such a situation the relieving pitcher is allowed as much time as he wants to warm up. Don Wilson, Roberts's reliever, off whom Aaron had hit his 611th home run, said later that as he stood on the mound it crossed his mind just to keep on warming up indefinitely, shaking his head and saying "No, not yet" to the umpires until night fell, and the moon came up, and perhaps at ten thirty the next morning some sort of statute of limitations would run out the season and he would be able to pack up and go home, sore-armed but relieved, to Houston, Texas.

The pitcher Jack Billingham would have done well to go to for advice is the tall, sidearmed whip-motion Dodger right-hander, Don Drysdale, now retired from active baseball and working as a broadcaster with the California Angels. Aaron hit the astonishing total of 17 home runs off him. Next down the line is Claude Osteen, who has been touched for 13. He is still active. He once said, "The last time I pitched against Aaron my dad came to the game. He took me aside: 'Don't let Aaron hit one off you.' Then he shook my hand and thought to say, 'Hello, son.' "

When Osteen's rotation comes up against the Braves,

Drysdale often calls him on the phone (the two were former teammates) to remind him that he'd be delighted to be taken off the hook for being Aaron's special patsy. ("Now Claude, don't let down. That record is within *reach*.")

Drysdale is predictably defensive about his past troubles with Aaron. He pointed out to me with the keen recall almost all ballplayers seem to have in regard to their personal statistics that in the first two years he faced Aaron (a total of 17 at-bats each year) he only gave up one hit—a triple up the alley in right center which beat him in a game in Milwaukee in the summer of 1957. Thus at the beginning of their rivalry Drysdale was holding Aaron to a sub-.100 batting average.

But then there were the bad years for Drysdale. Both in 1959 and 1963 Aaron hit four home runs off him. Drysdale never felt it was possible to establish much of a "book" on how to pitch to Aaron. "Besides, there never is any set way to pitch to a great hitter; if there were, he'd be hitting .220. He's one of those 'five fingers and a prayer on the ball' hitters."

"What does he look like to you at the plate?" I asked.

"I always used to think that he had a lot of Stan Musial in his stance. From the pitcher's mound they both seem to *coil* at you. The only sensible thing—if you couldn't get the manager to let you skip a turn against him—was to mix the pitches, and keep the ball low, and if you were pitching to spots, it was important to miss *bad.* If you missed *good,* and the ball got in his power alley, sometimes you were glad it went out of the park and was not banged up the middle."

Drysdale was just in awe of the concussive nature of Aaron's power. He told me about a 250-foot home run Aaron duck-hooked into the short "Chinese wall" screen in the Los Angeles Coliseum—so hard that Drysdale got a crick in his neck from turning abruptly to watch it go by. "It's bad enough to have him hit any home run off you—turning and looking and saying to yourself, 'My God, how far is *that* one going to go.' But with the Coliseum home run I ended up not only in mental anguish, but literally in physical *pain*."

"At least you're not around now," I said.

"I've seen what happens out at the ball park," he said. "It's a tough thing for a pitcher."

Jack Billingham had good reason to worry about Aaron—having already had some uncomfortable confrontations with him. For sure, he had struck him out with the bases loaded to end one game, but on the other hand, Aaron had hit four home runs off him in five years, including one which cost Billingham what would have been his first win as a Red, and another that beat him in ten innings.

The night before the game in the Cincinnati suburb of Delhi Billingham did not have much time to dwell on such things. Because of the tornadoes rampaging through the area, he spent the night sleeping on the floor of his "family" room in the basement. At about three o'clock that afternoon the rain had begun falling, turning soon into hail, with the hailstones getting larger, first the size of marbles, then golf balls. Billingham said that he'd never heard anything quite like the roar and smack of hail hitting the cars on the street outside. He picked up one in his front yard—though he could hardly believe it—that was *twice* the size of a golf ball. A neighbor called to say that a tornado had been seen over by the airport, five or six miles away. But then the weather cleared slightly and Billingham went up to his bedroom to take a nap—the Aaron confrontation the next day just barely on the edge of his consciousness and making him yawn. Still, he was somewhat uneasy about the weather. He looked out his bedroom window and on the horizon he saw a huge cloud, ink black, "kind of blowing in a circle."

Billingham had never seen a tornado. He was not sure that this was one. But then, as he ran down and stood in his yard with his wife, the cloud, ugly enough but not especially frightening, suddenly began to disappear, revealing in its place, like a sort of unveiling, the huge funnel of the tornado.

Moving somewhat erratically about five or six miles away it lasted about fifteen minutes or so, finally drawing its funnel up into itself.

Billingham never actually heard the tornado itself but the winds in Delhi were hard, and very gusty, and

the shingles of one house down the street began tearing off the roof. Upstairs Billingham let his father
sleep. He describes him as a very nervous and uneasy
person, given that day to fretting about Aaron and how
his son was going to do against him, and there was no
need to compound matters by introducing the sight of
a tornado funnel to him. They woke him up later on
when it was evening; he was hard to keep calm; the
tornado warnings were still on, and people in the neigh-
borhood sat on their porches, looking up at the sky.

Billingham slept on a mattress on the floor that night.
At dawn, he took his pillow and crept upstairs to get
a few more hours' sleep. The tornado warnings had
been lifted and the day was beautiful, with a sort of
snapping, cleansing wind blowing out of the southwest
—a wind that would give a lift to anything Aaron hit
toward left field in Riverfront Stadium.

In the Billingham household there continued to be
almost no talk about Aaron. His father, looking at the
faces around the breakfast table, said that he had heard
there had been earthquakes around the area. He got on
the subject of Aaron only once, and Billingham said,
"Dad, just cool it. I'm going out there to do my best.
If I have a bad day, please don't get upset about it."

He got to the ball park about ten thirty. The only
damage he could see from the tornado was four telephone poles which were down by the road along the
river. As he walked into the stadium he began to get
the flutters for the first time.

The Hitter

On occasion, as Henry Aaron sits in the
Braves' dugout, he takes off his baseball cap and holds
it close against his face. He moves it around until he
is able to peer through one of the ventholes in the
crown of the cap at the opposing pitcher on the mound.
The practice, like focusing through a telescope, serves

to isolate the pitcher, setting him apart in a round frame so that Aaron can scrutinize him and decide how he will deal with him once he reaches the plate.

The thought process he goes through during this is to decide what sort of pitch during his stand at the plate he will almost surely see . . . engraving this possibility in his mind's eye so that when the pitch comes (almost as if dictating what he wants) he can truly rip at it. Home-run hitters must invariably be "guessers," since their craft depends on seeing a pitch come down that they *expect*—so they have time to generate a powerful swing. More than one pitcher had said that Aaron seems to hop on a pitch as if he had called for it. Ron Perranoski, an ex-Dodger relief pitcher who in his first six seasons against Aaron held him to an .812 average (13 for 16), once said: "He not only knows what the pitch will be, but *where* it will be."

Aaron describes his mental preparation as a process of elimination. "Suppose a pitcher has three good pitches—a fast ball, a curve, and a slider. What I do, after a lot of consideration and analyzing and studying, is to eliminate two of those pitches, since it's impossible against a good pitcher to keep all three possibilities on my mind at the plate. So in getting rid of two, for example, I convince myself that I'm going to get a fast ball down low. When it comes, I'm ready. Now I can have guessed *wrong,* and if I've set my mind for a fast ball it's hard to do much with a curve, short of nibbling it out over the infield. But the chances are that I'll eventually get what I'm looking for."

The procedure of "guessing" has many variants. Roger Maris, for one, went up to the plate always self-prepared to hit a fast ball, feeling that he was quick enough to adjust to a different sort of pitch as it flew toward the plate. Most "guess" hitters play a cat-and-mouse game with the pitcher as the count progresses. What distinguishes Aaron's system is that once he makes up his mind what he will see during a time at bat he never deviates. He has disciplined himself to sit and wait for one sort of pitch whatever the situation.

One might suppose that a pitcher with a large repertoire of stuff would trouble Aaron—and that indeed turns out to be the case. He shakes his head when he thinks of Juan Marichal. "When he's at the prime of his game he throws a good fast ball, a good screwball, a good change-up, a good slider, a good you-have-it . . . and obviously the elimination system can't work; you can't throw out five or six different pitches in the hope of seeing one; the odds of seeing it would be too much against the batter."

What to do against a Marichal then? "It's an extra challenge," Aaron says. "I've just got to tune up my bat a little higher. It's a question of confidence, *knowing* that the pitcher cannot get me out four times without me hitting the ball sharply somewhere."

It is this confrontation between pitcher and hitter that fascinates Aaron, and indeed it is what he likes best about baseball—what he calls "that damn good guessing game."

Obviously there have been the bad times. His manager in the mid-1950s, Fred Haney, was thinking of benching him against Don Drysdale, who was giving him such fits in their early confrontations. "I had a psychological block going there. Drysdale was throwing from way out by third base with that sidearm motion of his, and he was mean, and it was hard to hang in there, knowing how mean he was; I had an awful lot of respect for him."

Haney finally decided to stick with Aaron, who fortuitously stroked the triple in Milwaukee, his first hit off Drysdale, which both pitcher and batter have remembered with such clarity since it established a balance of mutual respect.

"So much of it has to do with concentration," Aaron explained to me. "On the day of a night game I begin concentrating at four in the afternoon. Just before I go to bat, from the on-deck circle, I can hear my little girl—she's 12 now—calling from the stands, 'Hey daddy! Hey, daddy!' After the game she says to me, 'Hey, you never look around, daddy, to wave.' Well, sometimes I look at her, I can't help it, but not too often. I'm looking at the pitcher. I'm thinking very hard about him."

His discipline is so extreme that not only does Aaron

not hear anything when he gets to the plate, simply sealed in his vacuum of concentration, but his habits are so strictly adhered to that over the years he has never seen one of his home runs land in the stands. He is too busy getting down the first-base line.

I said I couldn't believe him. I must have sounded petulant about it because his brown eyes looked at me quickly.

"What I mean is," I said, "that I can't imagine denying oneself the pleasure of seeing the results of something like that. I mean it's like finishing a painting with one grand stroke of the brush and not stepping back to look at it."

I knew that most players do watch the home runs drop, at least the long ones, dawdling just out of the batter's box on that slow trot, the head turned. In the films of Bobby Thomson's Miracle home run in 1951 against the Dodgers in the playoffs at the Polo Grounds, it is quite apparent, his face in profile, that he glories in the drive going in; in fact, he does a small hop of delight halfway down the first-base line.

"Well, that's not what I'm supposed to do," Aaron was saying. "I've seen guys miss first base looking to see where the ball went. My job is to get down to first base and touch it. Looking at the ball going over the fence isn't going to help. I don't even look at the home runs in batting practice. No sense to break a good habit."

The odd thing about Aaron's attitude at the plate is that there is nothing to suggest any such intensity of purpose. His approach is slow and lackadaisical. He was called "Snowshoes" for a time by his teammates for the way he sort of pushes himself along. He carries his batting helmet on his way, holding two bats in the other hand. He stares out at the pitcher. He drops the extra bat. Then, just out of the batting box, resting his bat on the ground with the handle end balanced against his thighs, he uses both hands to jostle the helmet correctly into position. He steps into the box. Even here there is no indication of the kinetic possibility—none of the ferocious tamping of his spikes to get a good toehold that one remembers of Willie Mays, say, and the quick switching of his bat back and forth as he waits. Aaron steps into the batter's box as if he were going to sit down in it somewhere. His attitude is such that Robin Roberts, the Phillies pitcher, once explained, "That's why you can't fool Aaron. He falls asleep between pitches."

Jim Brosnan, ex-pitcher and author of the fine baseball chronicle *The Long Season,* once told me, "It was odd pitching to him. I always had a lot of confidence—perhaps because he walked up the way he did and because he stood so far away from the plate, just as far away as he could. That made you think that he wasn't fearless, which is good for a pitcher's morale. It looked as though he was giving away the outside of the plate to the pitcher, like he didn't want to stand in there and protect it. Still, I gave up two home runs to him. Funny, I don't remember one of them at all. I must have made a mistake, which I have made so many of that I tend to forget. But the other I remember because it was made off a perfect pitch, right in that classic spot where you're supposed to pitch to him, and he reached over, and those wrists of his snapped, and it was gone. I was so startled that I thought I'd thrown a bad pitch. When I got back to the dugout, I asked Hal Smith, who was my catcher, and he said right off that it could not have been improved on.

"I'm sure there're all sorts of stories like that. I remember once that Dick Sisler, the pitcher, came over to us from the American League in a winter trade and he sort of scoffed at those Aaron tales we told him. When you have someone like Aaron in your league you spend a lot of time bragging about him—perhaps so that when he hits a home run you can slough it off: 'I told you so; see?' Well, Sisler didn't believe any of this stuff. He kept telling us what it was like to pitch to Mickey Mantle, how *he* was the sort of guy who really scared you when he stood in the batter's box. Finally, in the exhibition season, Sisler got a chance to pitch to Aaron. The game was in Bradenton, Florida, and on Sisler's first pitch to him, a breaking ball, Aaron hit a foul line drive over the clubhouse, which is 450 feet away. It went out there on the line—just a terrible thing for any pitcher to see, even if it was foul. At the end of the inning Sisler came back to the dugout and he was saying, 'All right. All right. OK. OK'—like you say when you're convinced and you don't want to hear about it no more."

Dixie Walker, who was a Braves' batting coach at one time, and National League batting champion in 1944, used to stand in the shower and gaze at Aaron, his body glistening in the steam across the room, to try to figure out where this sort of power came from. "There's nothing you can tell by his size," he once said. "All I know is that he has the best wrists I've ever seen on a batter. He swings the bat faster than anyone else, it's as simple as that, and that's why the ball *jumps* the way it does."

That was what the baseball people marveled at when they talked about Aaron's batting—his wrists, the strength and quickness of them which produced a home-run trajectory like that of a good four-iron shot in golf—line drives quite unlike the towering lofty shots of a Mantle or Babe Ruth, whose blasts very often were coming straight down when they dropped out of the sky into the seats.

Bob Skinner, who coaches the Pittsburgh Pirates in the National League, once described the trajectory of an Aaron home run with convincing clarity: "The ball starts out on a line and the shortstop jumps for it, just over his fingertips, and then the left fielder jumps for it, just over *his* glove, and the ball keeps rising on that line and whacks up against the slats of a seat in the stands. The two fielders both figured they had a chance of catching that ball, except none of them realized how fast it was rising."

This reminds one, of course, of the famous hyperbolic description of a Rogers Hornsby home run which went between the pitcher's legs and kept on rising in a line over second base and then the center fielder and, for all I know, out over the center-field clock. But I have heard any number of players say they have seen infielders leap for an Aaron hit powered by those incredible wrists that went out on a line and landed beyond the wall.

"What an advantage it is to have great wrists," Hank Greenberg once told me. "It means that you don't have to commit until the last possible second, and yet you're still able to generate full power. How often you hear catchers say, 'I thought the ball was in my glove and the son of a bitch flicked it out of there for a home run.' "

The best example of Aaron's wrist power that the older Braves could remember was his performance back in 1964 during a demonstration of a weird-looking machine called an Iso-Swing. Developed as a teaching-aid for hitters, it was a six-feet-tall structure with rubber arms stretched over the strike zone above the plate. The theory was that the batter could stand up to this machine and develop and refine the power and style of his swing by practicing until he could consistently pop his bat through. This machine was wheeled up to Aaron and a number of the Braves during practice one day in Milwaukee.

Aaron was the first to try it. He stepped up and striding forward, he popped his first swing clearly through the confluence of rubber arms. Some eyebrows went up, and technicians (I've always imagined them in the white smocks typical of auto testing commercials) bent to the machine and tightened up some screws. Aaron swung his bat and did it successfully three more times.

Joe Adcock, the Braves' first baseman, then tried it. He was a truly powerful man, no one to fuss with in a barroom showdown, or in arm wrestling, or in *anything* involving strength . . . and Adcock flexed every muscle he had and with a grunt he swung his bat into the rubber apparatus. It was as if he had swung his bat against a thick tree. Frank Torre (who told me about this) said he half expected Adcock to straighten up and start vibrating like a cartoon character who has run into a shut door.

I asked Torre what would happen if a pitcher hung ten curve balls to Aaron and those wrists.

"It'd be like laying a lollipop up there. Or a big ol' melon. He'd hit five of them downtown. A batter like

Pete Rose, who controls the bat as well as he does, well, he would hit eight of those ten for base hits."

I whistled.

"That's some feat," he agreed. "Hitting is the toughest thing in all sports. The pitch comes down and in two-fifths of a second the hitter must decide if the ball is going to be in the strike zone and whether it's going to be a fast ball or a curve. Aaron is just the best ever who works at that for a profession. And nothing seems to be slowing him down."

The Hitter

The night before the opener some reporter asked him the classic sportswriter question: What had he had to eat the night before?

A piece of fish, Aaron had said.

The reporter wrote that down. So did some others. Some of them began to complain that they were getting the same answers; it was pointed out that they were asking the same questions.

Aaron said about it, "The reporters rush in and ask questions—mostly about hitting. Now we're into the food questions—some silly thing like how many shrimp can I eat at a sitting. Then they rush out again; then I read that I'm 'mysterious,' or 'not colorful,' or 'full of grave silence.' "

It was the only time I heard him even mildly querulous about the press of questions and the almost stultifying smother of reporters. He worried about the effect it was having on his teammates. Above the ramp from the locker room down to the field in Atlanta was a sign that read "We Are All in This Together," which must have seemed slightly paradoxical considering the slavish attention he got. His teammates shrugged. From the openings of their cubicles it must have looked as if

Aaron in his area was holding a high-stakes craps game on the floor, completely out of sight, with a ring of people standing on their tiptoes to see.

Out on the field the press of reporters was like a bee swarm. When Aaron moved from the dugout to the batting cage they pressed in around him so that it was only possible to see his blue and white cap amid the crush and the cameras being aimed unseen, with the hands up and the fingers busily working at the shutters, and he was only able to emerge from this when he stepped into the privacy of the batting cage.

He didn't seem to let on that it was a bother. He seemed to have an instinct and an ease, though obviously not a man of pretensions, for finding simple yet graceful answers. I remember on the last day of the 1973 season someone at his final press conference asked him what "good" he had done for baseball. It was such a surprising question that a murmur of dismay drifted around the room and Aaron himself said, "That's a new one," and then he said with just a touch of scorn, "I haven't done a thing for it."

He turned away for an instant, but then he came back to the question, as if it were improper not to make an attempt at it. "Maybe what I've done is make new fans," he said quietly. "At first there was a lot of mail from people, older people, who didn't want me to break Babe Ruth's record. The young generation took note of that, and supported me. I think they want to relate to me, to see me have a record, not someone their granddad saw play."

He was getting precisely the kind of attention that was such a burden to Roger Maris in *his* chase of Ruth's record of 60 home runs in a year. But Maris couldn't adapt to the situation. He was a country boy from Fargo, North Dakota, which has a smaller population than the capacity of Yankee Stadium. He valued his privacy to such a degree that he used to say that even in Fargo he didn't know his next-door neighbor. He fretted. He worried about his toeholds at the plate; he used exactly the same toeholds dug in the batter's box by Tony Kubek, who preceded him in the order, and when his hitting sagged slightly, he took Kubek out to the plate with a tape measure to check that Tony had not unwittingly changed his stance slightly. "Really, I'm not comfortable. What's going on? Aren't you digging those holds in the same place?" He began ducking the world: "I go to my apartment and stay there," he said in one memorable statement. "It's very interesting, if you like the inside of apartments."

Joe Garagiola, the former player now broadcasting for NBC, once analyzed it as follows: "A ballplayer becomes famous and he's invited on a banquet circuit and everyone expects him to tell funny stories. Well, very often he *can't* . . . but he never gets any benefit of the doubt. Roger Maris was a good journeyman ballplayer who slowly moved into a limelight as he got closer to Ruth's record, and at the end, right in the cone of light, there was nothing in his makeup to allow him to handle it. He stayed the same. That's the way he was. And my God he hated it. He was just seething inside. His hair started to fall out."

The year of the 61 home runs literally changed Maris, and he vowed he would never go through such an experience again. He altered his batting style the year following the record and began to punch the ball: his home-run production dropped from 61 to 33.

But as for Aaron, Joe Garagiola was astonished by his calm in the vortex of it all. "It's like what happens to ballplayers at World Series time. They come out of the dugout on the way to the batting cage and the reporters come alongside and ask, 'How do you feel?' They get asked the *same* question when they step out of the batting cage, 'How do you feel?' every two steps, and finally it gets to them: they go back in the locker room and look in the mirror to see how they *do* feel. Not Aaron. It just doesn't seem to bother him."

He did a television interview with Aaron in which, being interested in the crazier questions put to Aaron, Garagiola had the two of them reverse roles.

Garagiola: You be the sportscaster. You ask me the questions that they've been asking you. OK?

Aaron: OK. Here's the first one. "What did you do

to make your wrists strong?" That's the number one question.

Garagiola: Throwing spitballs in school—that is a surefire way to build up strength in your wrists. No, what *is* truly the answer to that?

Aaron: Actually it was carrying blocks of ice up two or three flights of steps with a pair of tongs.

Garagiola: Ask me another.

Aaron: "Do you put your left shoe on first, or the right?"

Garagiola: Somebody really asked you that?

Aaron: During the all-star game. I said he could come in the locker room and watch for himself.

Garagiola: And watch you . . .

Aaron: That's right. The big one is about the pressure. "Do you feel any pressure?"

Garagiola: I don't sleep. I don't eat much. I feel scratchy. I choke . . .

Aaron: That's what they'd *like* me to say. That's why they keep asking me—in the hope I'll back down and admit that to them.

Garagiola: Do you have a different answer for each time you're asked—just to keep it interesting?

Aaron: No. I tell them that there's really not too much pressure. I can take two or three years to beat the Ruth record.

Garagiola: That's true.

Aaron: Here's another. "What size bat do you use?" "I use a 33½-ounce bat." They say, "You mean you use a bat that *light*?" I say, "Yep, 33½ ounces." So they pick up my bat and swing it around, and heft it, and they say, "Well, wait a minute. This thing must weigh thirty-*five* . . ."

Garagiola: Like they know.

Aaron: There was this one guy who said to me, "Hank, I've been following your career for a long time, and I've noticed the progress you've made, which is great, and I wanted to know which way do you bat—left or right?"

Garagiola: Oh, now, you're puttin' me on. Somebody asked you that?

Aaron: Somebody asked me which way did I hit.

Garagiola: Is that the most unusual question they've asked you?

Aaron: Well, I get a lot of requests for a piece of my hair. People want it sent through the mail.

Garagiola: That's why *I'm* like this. [Garagiola is very high-domed indeed.] I kept sendin' my hair out.

Aaron: Joe, when you played, did you ever imagine yourself challengin' Babe Ruth's home-run record?

Garagiola: Henry, if I took all my home runs, including the three I hit on the playground, and multiplied by *nine,* I'd still be 28 short. No, I never thought I'd challenge Babe Ruth's record.

Aaron: I tried to catch one of your home runs, you know.

Garagiola: You're kiddin'?

Aaron: No . . .

Garagiola: Where?

Aaron: In Pittsburgh.

Garagiola: Look right at the camera and tell 'em.

Aaron: I tried to catch one of your home runs in Pittsburgh.

Garagiola: How far was it?

Aaron: About 380.

Garagiola: Look in the camera. How far?

Aaron: About 380.

Garagiola: 380. And the wind was blowin' in?

Aaron: Blowin' in. Yeah!

Garagiola: And you thought you could catch it?

Aaron: Yeah.

Garagiola: And you jumped up?

Aaron: Jumped up.

Garagiola: Tell 'em that it was hit hard.

Aaron: It was hit hard.

Garagiola: You didn't wanna catch it because you might hurt your hand.

Aaron: I was *afraid* it was gonna hurt my hand.

Garagiola: Yeah, and you wouldn't be able to play again.

Aaron: Right.

Garagiola: Right?

Aaron: Right.

The Observer

Not long after my writer friend and I arrived at the stadium we noted a number of men standing around with translucid tubes that ran up into an ear from the collar of their long tan raincoats . . . secret service men wearing some new-fangled intercom apparatus. They were on hand to look out for the vice-president who was scheduled to throw out the first ball. ("Who's Jerry Ford?" one Braves' official was reported to have asked, not making the connection.)

As we were going up in one of the elevators one of these men standing in the corner suddenly erupted into voice, "Get out! Get out! Stop this elevator. Everybody must get out!"

Apparently some order had drifted up the tube into his ear—presumably that the official party had arrived and the elevator was to be commandeered for them.

"Get out! Let's move!"

My writer friend peered over. He was in the back of the elevator. "Who the hell are you to be ordering us around in this elevator?"

"Secret service."

"Well, dammit, announce yourself as such. Don't order us. *Ask* us."

He stood outside the elevator quaking with anger, and as the door closed on the operator and the secret service man behind, looking out balefully, he cried in, "Civility; learn some goddam civility." I thought he was going to bang on the closed door.

He set up his typewriter in the press section. It was going to take him a long time to wind down. The section was glassed in, and soundproof so that the sounds of the crowd filing in, and the players in their pregame practice went unheard and it was like looking down on some mysterious pantomime from a glass-bottom boat. I went down into the stands. The wind swirled around, picking up napkins and fluttering them between the seats. Someone said that the wind wouldn't make any difference in the case of a long Aaron fly to left since its force was dissipated into meaningless swirls by the contours of the stadium. Others weren't so sure. The flags pointed directly to left, snapping like the sails of a boat coming up into a stiff wind. Billingham came out to warm up alongside the stands. A gust of wind caught him during his wind-up and nearly toppled him over.

Aaron's family arrived an hour before game time. They were seated just off the Braves' dugout on the third-base side—among them his wife Billye and his father, who had come up from Mobile. Aaron's father is a solemn-faced man with small chiseled features; a red-tipped kitchen match stuck at a high angle out of his mouth. Someone asked him a question about Babe Ruth and he put the match in his top pocket. He said he had seen Babe Ruth hit a home run during an exhibition game in Mobile. "I climbed a pine tree outside the ball park to see him. He sure hit the ball. They tell the story that the ball went over the fence into a freight car on a train going by and they found the ball in New Orleans. That was four or five years before Henry was born."

A man with a strong Arkansas accent leaned over and asked him for his autograph. Mr. Aaron put the matchstick back in his mouth and signed the scrap of paper and said, "Thank you, sir."

Someone asked him if he had been prepared for his son's run at the record. "I never paid the record no attention," he said. "It slipped up on me like everybody else. Henry was in baseball for *work*."

The Ball

I decided to watch the opener from the left-field seats to see what the excitement out there would be if the home-run ball happened to drop in. The amounts offered by various concerns for the baseballs were considerable—those for the number 715 ball seemed to go up weekly—from $11,111 offered by two Greene County Georgians (who said they wanted to keep the ball in Georgia somewhere) to $15,000 from a Baltimore businessman, Julio Gonzalez, to finally a $25,000 offer put up by an anonymous fan in Venezuela. Out in the left-field stands was a man called Jurgens who represented the Stacey Storage and Moving Company. He was offering $2,000 for 714, and $12,000 on the spot to anyone who brought him 715. I ran into him out there, flanked by two special policemen.

I asked him about the mysterious Venezuelan fan who had offered $25,000.

Jurgens looked scornful. "Would you hunt for someone in Venezuela offering $25,000 or take $12,000 on the spot? I've got it right here."

As the two policemen seemed to wedge in against him a bit, he showed me a thick sheaf of 120 hundred-dollar bills in his inside coat pocket. The pocket was secured by a safety pin.

"I've got thirty men in the stands—they're the ones in red jackets, my daughter with them. We're really pulling for him to put the ball up in here because we really think we have a crack at ending up with it."

All of this interest in the ball, obviously, meant that it had to be carefully marked so that when the tying and winning home runs were hit, the actual ball could be properly identified. The Braves' management were worried that dozens of people would turn up at the clubhouse waving baseballs and clamoring for rewards. Each ball was stamped with invisible ink—last year with a diamond with the number of the upcoming home run within, this year with two sets of numbers, a marked pattern that lit up under a small fluorescent lamp which Bill Acree, the Braves' equipment manager, packed along to Cincinnati in one of the team trunks.

"We don't want any mistakes," Acree said. "Excitement over this is so damn intense."

Even the ballplayers began to be affected, especially those on the opposing teams who had no sense of obligation to deliver the ball back to Aaron. Schemes were plotted. Some speculated that if at one of his at-bats Aaron hit a soft single to the outfield, a venal and unscrupulous center fielder, say, could trap the ball, and then fall heavily, to rise slowly, holding his shoulder, crying out in apparent pain and obviously disoriented, stumbling here and there, while Aaron circled the bases for what the official scorer would have to call an inside-the-park home run. It would be a ruse worth the appalling amount of money if he could get away with it and manage to hang on to the ball on his way to the dugout.

I had been down into the umpires' room to watch them get ready for the game. They were sitting at a table plucking baseballs out of their red Spalding boxes and rubbing them up with the traditional Delaware River mud especially packed for the purpose, and provided in its large ribbed can before every game by the home-club since a new ball, right out of its package, is too slick for a pitcher to handle properly. The umpires shine up six to seven dozen for a ball game—four dabs of mud is the usual procedure, with sometimes a lick of spit, and the men, sitting in their undershirts, turn them in their big palms and set them aside on the tables. Bill Acree had already stamped two dozen balls with his marking device under the watchful eye of the umps. He supposed (he told me once) that they were on the watch to see that he didn't *palm* one of them, and substitute a rabbit ball.

"Now where does one go to buy a rabbit ball?" he asked me. "I've heard of 'rabbit balls' all my life, but if you challenged me to go out and find one, I'd be real stuck."

The procedure with the balls marked up in the umpires' room was that they would be introduced into the game every time Aaron came to bat. Last year the plate umpire had a special pouch on his belt for them; this year Bill Acree issued a ball, one at a time, from the Braves' dugout to the closest base umpire, who then tossed it to the pitcher. All of this could not do much to help the pitcher's confidence—the scurrying preparations of those attending to an execution. Last year, Juan Marichal saw this activity, the plate umpire reaching in the special ball bag at his waist, and not being aware of the procedure felt that he was the victim of some odd plot, that perhaps the ball he would get from the umpire was going to pop in two and emit smoke as he gripped it for his screwball.

The big topic of conversation among the umpires was not so much the preparation for the Aaron home run as the problems with the cowhide baseballs which, because of a shortage of horsehide, had been introduced into the leagues earlier that spring. Apparently because of inferior stitching, the balls on occasion flew apart, the covers literally knocked off. I asked Ed Vargo, who was the chief of the crew, which was the operative part of the ball if it became thus unraveled, bouncing out across the infield and affording the infielder a *choice,* and he said, with complete solemnity, "You go with the *core* in such a case."

I was curious about what would his emotions be if Aaron hit number 714.

"I will watch home plate to make sure he touches it," Vargo said. "It will be a thrill, a great thrill, of course, but we're not supposed to throw our caps up into the air. So I'll stand by the plate and watch him come to it. That's what my job is."

"Suppose he's carried off the base paths to a distant restaurant, say, on the shoulders of exultant fans?" I said.

"Common sense prevails," Vargo said firmly. "The fault is not his."

"He doesn't have to struggle a bit?"

"In Pittsburgh in 1960 Mazeroski was carried all over the field when he homered that time and I don't know if he ever did get to home plate."

The Pitcher

Billingham started the game badly. He walked the Braves' lead-off hitter, Ralph Garr, on four

straight pitches, and then he gave up a single to Mike
Lum. Darrell Evans flied to left field, and Billingham
heard the roar that meant that Aaron in his lazy-
seeming fashion was moving up from the on-deck circle.
Perhaps shaken by what he was looking at in the batter's box Billingham missed the plate on his first two
pitches, and then he gained a little confidence by throwing a strike past Aaron, but his next pitch was another
ball. His fifth pitch was supposed to be a fast ball,
thrown for the outside corner. Normally, Billingham's
fast ball behaves a little like a sinker, but in this case
it sailed in—not a bad pitch, Billingham was later to
admit ruefully, "but it was too good a pitch for Henry
Aaron."

Aaron swung his bat for the first time in the 1974
season and the ball rose on a line for the left center-
field seats, Rose running for the fence, with Rettenmund circling behind him in case the ball rebounded off
the fence.

Billingham said to himself, "Oh, my God. I did it."
He couldn't believe what had happened. He heard the
roar. He turned around; he vaguely remembers putting
his hands on his knees, bending over in disgust, cursing,
and then he looked up in time to see the ball go over
the fence.

"I thought I might as well watch it. I knew it was a
record, of course, but what I remembered mainly was
that here it was the first inning of the season and I was
behind three runs."

The ceremonies began behind home plate. Billingham
continued to throw, keeping his arm warm and trying
to dismiss the past. He heard Aaron saying over the
loudspeaker system, "I certainly would like to thank
you very much and I'm just glad it's almost over with."

Suddenly everything about the ceremony seemed a
personal taunt, his own presence completely foolish as
the cluster of celebrants continued to mill in tight
around Aaron. It became an affront to be ignored, his
mistake being gloried over and relished by the entire
ball park, the Cincinnati fans included. He began to
throw the ball with increasing velocity to his catcher
Johnny Bench, calling out quite audibly, perhaps even

enough for the vice-president and the commissioner and other well-wishers to hear, "Let's get going. Let's go!" He stomped around the pitcher's mound mumbling that first they had changed the ball on him, giving him one covered with invisible ink, *that* was bothersome, and now *this* ceremony—all of it calculated to throw off his rhythm. He wanted to pitch to Dusty Baker, that's what he wanted to do. He'd had more success against him.

When time was called back in, he pitched much better than he expected. He retired the side, and walked toward the Red dugout. When he sat down he noticed Clay Kirby, another member of the pitching staff, staring at him curiously; he suddenly realized the enormity of the home run he had given up . . . that not only had it tied the Ruth record, but inconceivably it had been hit over the fence on Aaron's first swing of the season.

"I didn't waste any time, did I?" Billingham said.

The Ball

Circling the outfield at Riverfront Stadium is a 12-feet-high solid fence enclosing an area between it and the stadium wall—as narrow, dark, and untidy as a city alleyway, sunless, with the ground littered with beer cups, programs, hot-dog wrappers and wrinkled balloons, swaying slowly, their buoyancy gone. In the officialese spoken by the Cincinnati Reds' functionaries it is called "the void territory." Colloquially, it is referred to as "the pit." The Cincinnati management had entombed a pair of policemen down in there and some ground-crew attendants. The policemen (Clarence Williams and Steve Halpin) were told to act as "deterrents" to fans who might try to jump into the "pit" and scale the fence to reach the playing field itself. They were not given any instruction as to what to do if a baseball sailed into their enclosure. Neither was pleased with the assignment. Looking straight up they could see a patch of sky, a sort of Wall Street canyon view. It was possible to read the scoreboard with its countless computations, animated cartoons, and such announcements as "Greetings to the Netherland Rubber Company." Observing the scoreboard and listening to the crowd noise swell and ebb above them gave both at least some sense of what was going on.

But most of the time the two men stood with their backs to the wall, looking up at the thin patch of sky, and commiserated with each other about the lunacy of having volunteered for the stadium detail—it being an off-duty day for both—in the hopes of seeing an historic game, and then being stuck down in a trench by their superiors.

"Not even a knothole," Williams told me later. "Just a wall to look at and you knew that just beyond it was Rose . . . and Rettenmund . . . and Aaron . . . just a few *yards* away—the most frustrating damn thing."

In the top half of the first inning Williams heard the great roar go up and glancing up at the busy board above him he saw that under "At Bat" there was the number 44.

"I positioned myself," he said, "just in case."

A moment or so later, with a 3 under the "Balls" sign on the board and a 1 under "Strikes," Williams heard the distant pop and the quick tumult of sound.

"Everybody above us jumped up and down and began bellowing, and over the fence appeared the *ball,* just like that, and it bounced in the mud in front of me, spattering my pants, and came to me on one bounce."

"Did you think of the reward?" I asked him.

"Oh, there was a small temptation to run out of the park with it. I knew there was money offered off it . . . But if I could have done it all over again, I mean if I was back there, looking up, and the ball came over the fence, I would have kept it—but only so I could have presented it to Aaron myself. That was the big disappointment—that I didn't get a chance to deliver the ball to him. What happened was that the ball came over the fence and as soon as I had it in my hand this attendant came rushing at me with this open paper *bag* . . . 'Drop it in here! Drop it in here! . . .' and I did.

They opened up a gate in the wall and there were 56,000 people and out walked this guy with my ball in a paper bag and two guards on either side and they kept right on going to the infield and gave the ball to the president of the National League and eventually it got to Aaron via the vice-president of the United States! It would have been great to be involved in all of that. But damn, they shut me up in the "pit," closed the gate on me, and I didn't even see the ceremony."

They stood out there for most of the game. In the sixth inning, hearing a big sustained yell high in the left-field stands, they guessed that either a fight was going on, or more likely (which turned out to be the case) that baseball was being inflicted with its first streaker of the season. From time to time reporters circled the outfield stands and got onto the platform used for some of the standing-room crowds at the Cincinnati Bengals' football games. From this promontory they could peer into the pit at Williams and the rest of his detail and shout their questions down through cupped hands much as if they were interviewing people trapped in a well:

"Which one of you guys caught the ball?"

"What about the paper bag? Where did that come from?"

"Did you catch it on the fly? I said, *'Did you catch it on the fly?'* "

"Where's the guy who had the paper bag?"

"Who's the guy with you? Halpin? Is that how you spell it, H-A-L-P-I-N?"

And so forth.

Williams finally got his chance to meet Aaron. He was introduced to the reporters at Aaron's postgame press conference, the room bright with television lights, and he stood in there blinking his eyes, his smile quick and friendly under his small moustache. The Cincinnati police wear high-lidded hats with white crowns, like the sort of caps firemen wear in parades, which seems to endow their owners with pleasant dispositions. He was delighted with the fuss and attention. When asked how old he was, he grinned and lapsed into police-ese: "Three one fifty-two, that's my birthday," and the reporters' lips moved as they wrote the figures down and did their subtracting.

Aaron was led in dressed in a gabardine suit. At first he was nonplussed by finding the policeman apparently sharing the spotlight with him; it was explained to him. "Oh, thank you," he said to Williams and the two shook hands. The camera flashlights began to pop.

The Observer

The Reds' locker room is so fastidiously decorated in chartreuse—red carpets, chairs, locker facings—that it glows like a cocktail lounge. It was almost deserted when I walked in; some of the players were down in a room at one end watching Aaron at his press conference on television; others were in the showers. They had won the game 7-6 and while everybody else was thinking of Aaron's home run, they were exulting in there.

At one end of the lounge was a framed signboard illuminated by a bulb within. The message on it, in black block letters, read WHAT YOU SAY HERE/WHAT YOU SEE HERE/LET IT STAY HER (the final E had disappeared). Some wag had signed the bottom frame with a felt-tip pen, "Very truly yours . . . Jim Bouton"—in reference to the ex-Yankee pitcher's lively kiss-and-tell book, *Ball Four*.

I read the cork-backed notice board. An announcement on Reds' stationery stated that 30 college editors had been invited to the game that afternoon and some of them might be venturing onto the field during batting practice. "You will have little trouble recognizing them," the announcement read. "They'll be more timid than your average newsman. Six are female."

I dropped by the locker of Tony Perez, the Reds' first baseman, the first person Aaron had met in his tour of the bases. Last year the Astros' first baseman,

Lee May, had plotted to surprise Aaron if he hit 714 in the last day of the season by grabbing him in a big bear hug as he came down the first-base line; while congratulating him enthusiastically he was planning to reach up and swipe his batting helmet. He knew that in the press of the moment it was unlikely that Aaron would struggle over it. The helmet would end up on a peg in his trophy room in Houston and he would nod at it, if there was company, and say, "Well, there it is, Bad Henry's batting helmet, the one he wore when he hit 714 . . ."

I asked Perez if he had devised any such plot. He smiled broadly and said he wished he'd thought of something like that. He had missed the boat. He had begun to put out his hand. He wanted to say "Congratulations," but he only had time to say ". . . eh, Henry," and Aaron was on his way to second.

No sign of Billingham. I looked in on Don Gullett. He was scheduled to pitch against Aaron on Saturday. He was sitting on a stool in front of his locker in his undershorts. He has the young fresh face of the marine who appears in the first reel of a World War II movie and dies almost immediately in the dunes behind the beachhead—an impression fortified by the pitcher's slight stature, like a teen-ager's: only his fingers seemed outsized, long and graceful. He held a cork-tipped cigarette and puffed at it. His heels, in sandals, jiggled up and down. 715. Much worse than 714.

He had had Aaron on his mind before; indeed Aaron had hit seven home runs off him, including an opening day home run in 1972. He affected considerable sang-froid: "It doesn't bother me, any of this. It's going to happen sooner or later. No, I'm not going to treat it different than any other game."

What had he learned about pitching to Aaron since that opening day home run in Riverfront?

He didn't look up at his questioners. He stared out straight ahead. "I *pitch* more to him now, rather than challenging him. I've thrown two by him . . ." He paused and tapped his cigarette.

"What happened to the third?" I asked.

His eyes looked up for the first time, but he didn't

smile; he took a puff, and then shifted on his stool.
"When the batter gets older his reflexes are supposed
to slow down," he said. "Throw it by them! I could do
that with Willie Mays when he was finishing. But
Aaron . . . even if you *think* you have it by him, those
great wrists of his flick it out of the catcher's mitt . . . I
swear that's what it seems like. You know something,
I'm trying to be cool. The more you think about it,"
he said, "the more you think about it."

The Observer

Gullett never had a chance to pitch to him
that day. The Braves' management decided not only
to keep Aaron out of the lineup on Saturday but also
on Sunday, the last day of the series. The officials said
that surely Aaron had satisfied the people in Cincinnati
by hitting number 714. Now it was the turn of the
home folk in Atlanta where the team was to open its
home stand on Monday night.
     The decision once again fanned up the controversy
which had first developed last winter when the Braves
announced that they planned to keep Aaron out of
the Cincinnati series entirely. The rationale was that
Aaron himself would prefer to try for the epochal home
runs before the hometown fans, and he owed them
that for their support over the years. After all, he didn't
play every game. He sat out 41 games in 1973. Why
not the first three of 1974?
     As soon as the action was announced, the sports-
writers' corps from New York—Dave Anderson and
Red Smith of the *Times*, Larry Merchant of the
Post, and especially Dick Young of the *News*, who
considers himself (so his colleagues say) to be the
"conscience of baseball"—rose up to attack the action
as crass, probably venal, and certainly tainted with
commercialism. The pursuit of the record was being

cheapened. It was being turned into a carnival attraction. They urged the commissioner of baseball, Bowie Kuhn, to do something about it.

To the dismay of the Braves' organization, and to the shrug-shouldered disgust of the Atlanta sportswriters who consider the commissioner a tool of the New York press, Bowie Kuhn made it quite clear that he expected the Braves to play Aaron in two out of the three games in Cincinnati—his view was that it was imperative that the public believe that every team always presents the strongest lineup in its best efforts to win. The New York writers rejoiced.

The reporters from the other camps weighed in. Furman Bisher of the *Atlanta Constitution* referred to New York as the "command post of charlatans," its sportswriters as "meddlesome Manhattan ice-agers," and advised them to clean up Times Square before taking on such lofty attitudes in criticizing others. He referred to Dick Young as "dishwater gray."

The New York writers defended the commissioner's decision on a less personal and somewhat higher plane, but they were nonetheless opinionated. Dave Anderson of the *Times* referred to the Braves' action as "a brazen defiance of baseball's integrity." Red Smith chimed in with a powerfully written description of Ted Williams on the last day of the 1941 season, who could have sat out the game and ended up with a .400 average, the first batter in the majors to reach that level in 11 years, the first in the American League in 18. He told how Joe Cronin offered Williams the day off, but the slugger wouldn't accept it and finished the day with six hits in eight times at bat, one of the hits so hard that it put a loudspeaker's horn out of operation. He ended up with a season average of .406. Red Smith ended his column with a terse one-line admonition: "That is how this game is played."

When Aaron hit his 714th home run, Red Smith's column the next morning had a headline which said that it was not only Aaron's finest hour, but Bowie Kuhn's for exercising his authority to get him into the lineup.

The following day, Saturday, just before the second

game of the series, Eddie Mathews called a press conference. He sat on top of the television set in his room, swinging his legs back and forth slightly. He has the big sloping shoulders of a fighter, and indeed he did quite a lot of fighting in his days in the National League, particularly in defense of a peppery teammate on the Braves named Johnny Logan. Logan had a peculiar knack of getting himself involved in fights where he was invariably outmatched, and Mathews came to his aid so often that he was known as John's "relief fighter."

Mathews indicated he was taking on the commissioner. He said that before the opening game the chairman of the board of the Braves, Bill Bartholomay, had asked him if the home-run record were not involved, would he play Aaron. Mathews had replied, "Yes, we would." Bartholomay shook his head and said, "Well, that answers our question."

But then (as Mathews put it), ". . . he hits the thing with his first swing of the bat. That changes my thinking. We've been fair enough."

Mathews announced that he would not play Aaron that afternoon or in the remaining game with the Reds on Sunday. The next time he would play would be in Atlanta. "Right or wrong, this is Eddie Mathews's decision."

The commissioner immediately found Mathews "wrong." He got on the phone after the game that afternoon and in so many words *ordered* the manager to insert Aaron in Sunday's final game of the series. He said that if Aaron did not play there would be "serious consequences."

"I asked what the consequences were," Mathews said in yet another press conference that evening. "He refused to say."

Once again the issue came down to fundamentals—whether baseball is a sport or a business, a conflict that Red Smith referred to as the wrangle between "the money changers and the Protectors of the Faith." The Braves' management talked about the aesthetics of Aaron hitting his 715th home run in his home ball park, and how the fans should be rewarded by seeing him do it, but they were also obviously thinking about drawing 400,000 people for a home stand in which the Braves would be playing 11 games in 13 days against the Dodgers, the Reds, and the Padres. If the "chase" were still on, the ball park would be packed.

But Mathews had no choice. In a signed statement he said:

> The commissioner has unlimited powers to impose very serious penalties on individuals or the ball club itself. For the first time I realize that these penalties are not only fines but also suspensions and other threats to the franchise itself.
>
> Because of this order and the threatened penalties, I intend to start Hank Aaron tomorrow.

There were both solemn and flippant arguments about the question. In what was possibly a normal reaction against traditionally authoritarian figures, most of the writers seemed to side with the Braves and against the commissioner and the New York writers. They argued that inserting a player into the lineup was not a matter for either the commissioner or the league president, or even a club owner . . . but surely the choice of the team's manager.

Somebody suggested that the next time the commissioner decided to make up a lineup card, it should include somebody truly interesting—Raquel Welch, for instance. Somebody else, who'd overheard this suggestion, offered one logical solution to the whole mess, namely, that Aaron could have solved everything and saved the home run for Atlanta by stepping up to the plate in Cincinnati with a 9-inch, 15-ounce bat. Could the commissioner have complained about this?

The commissioner himself was aware that his decision would outrage the citizens of Atlanta—to the extent that (he was to say much later) he felt he had better forget his plans to be on hand until Aaron hit 715. He had missed seeing Aaron get his 3,000th hit and 700th home run, but he had vowed to be in the stands for 715. He knew not being there would be seen as a cop-out, that his decision had been forced for fear of having rolled-up hot-dog wrappers scaled at him as he sat in his field box . . . but his feeling was firm, and probably justified . . . that his presence in Atlanta on opening day would refocus attention on the controversy and detract from the celebration if Aaron hit 715. "My presence would be a negative influence on what was supposed to be a positive occasion."

Throughout all this, Aaron himself adhered to the Braves' party line, though not vociferously. He said that he thought people should understand that baseball was a business. He had an additional sensible, if somewhat personal, view of the problem. He said that if he wanted to show his children the place where he broke Babe Ruth's record, he would like to step outside his front door in Atlanta and point at the great white doughnutlike structure on the hill outside the city ("That's where I did it."), rather than having to go out to the airport and take a plane to Cincinnati.

The Pitcher

How would it mark a man if he gave up number 715? Would he walk around shaken, forever saddled with the deed? Would people point at him in restaurants? It was an interesting point. Students of baseball know that it was Tom Zachary who pitched the ball that Ruth hit for his 60th home run in 1927, that Tracy Stallard gave up Maris's 61st home run in 1961, and that Guy Bush served up Ruth's 714th home run that spring day in Pittsburgh in 1935. But only the trivia experts would know that Ruth's 28th home run of the 1919 season (which broke the standing record of 27 owned by Edward Nagle Williamson) was given up by the Yankee pitcher Bob Shawkey. In 1921 Ruth broke Roger Connor's career record of 136 (the equivalent of Aaron surmounting 714); who would know that the pitcher was Dixie Davis of the St. Louis Browns?

But in fact the Ruth record was such an extraordinary one, and had been in existence for such a long time (the only one that Ruth himself thought would never be broken) that the newsmen collected in front of the cubicle of the pitcher scheduled against the Braves and gazed upon him as if he were condemned, addressing their questions to him in voices that seemed muted in sympathy. They knew that if he gave up the home run he was marked.

Perhaps there were some pitchers around the league who would not mind being identified with the eclipse of Ruth's record. Tracy Stallard, who was a young Boston Red Sox rookie when he gave up the 61st home run to Roger Maris, that broke Ruth's record of 60 in one year, afterward rather enjoyed the back-of-the-hand notoriety that came with being the victim of Maris's clout, and he would announce, to the point of volunteering, that he was the pitcher responsible. Most pitchers, though, were sensitive enough about their craft to feel differently about such a role. Ray Sadecki once said of Stallard, "I don't want to be him. Everybody knows *who* he is. Nobody knows *where* he is."

The pitcher most usually identified with a personal disaster on the mound is Ralph Branca, the Dodger pitcher who gave up the famous Miracle home run to Bobby Thomson in the 1951 playoff game that won the Giants the pennant. He is an insurance salesman now, in Binghamton, New York, and I was able to reach him by phone up there. He didn't appear to mind talking about what had happened.

"In fact if you asked me if I could strike that home run out of my life, I would say No. I'd rather have been involved with that thing. It's been beneficial." He began talking about the instant itself. He told me that Thomson had hit a fast ball thrown high and inside—what he intended as a waste pitch—hitting it with overspin, topping the ball slightly, and Branca kept crying inwardly, "Sink! Sink! Sink!" as he turned and watched the ball head for the seats. The motion pictures show him picking up the rosin bag behind the pitching rubber and throwing it down in disgust. Branca doesn't remember doing this. He recalls the long walk to the clubhouse steps in deep center field, being hardly aware of the commotion going on around him as his inner voice blared in horror at what he had done.

"It's a long walk. I don't think anyone walked with me."

I said that I remembered an extraordinary photograph taken of him in the clubhouse in which he was lying in his uniform face down on a flight of steps as if his grief had laid him out stiff as a length of cordwood.

"Yes," he said. "Those were the steps in the locker room that led up to a sort of alcove with lockers along the wall. The picture was taken by Barney Stein, who was a *New York Post* photographer. He was a great Dodger fan. All the other photographers had rushed over to the Giant locker room but he had stayed. The picture he took *before* the one you've remembered won him a big award—the Pulitzer prize, I think. It showed me sitting on the steps with my head down and my hands up and my fingers laced like I was trying to shut it all out. One reporter was still behind with Barney and when he asked some bugging question, I rolled over to get away from him, flat out, and Barney snapped the picture. It looks like I've stumbled on the bottom step and fallen full length on the steps."

"All this time—what was going on in your mind?" I asked somewhat tentatively—it seemed like such an excruciating experience to lead him through despite the twenty-odd years' lapse . . .

"I've described it, of course . . ." he said wearily.

"Yes."

"I kept wondering why it had happened to *me*. 'Why me? Why me?' I kept asking. I was a gung-ho all-American boy then. I lived the best life I could. I didn't drink or mess around. So I sat there and said to myself that there was no justice in life. I remember dressing finally and walking out to the parking lot where my fiancée was waiting in the car with Father

Pat Rawley, who was a dean at Fordham University. My fiancée saw me coming and burst into tears. I got into the car and I said, 'Why me? Why did it have to happen to me?' I really was frantic to know. Father Rawley leaned over the back seat and reminded me what Christ had realized from God: that He had been given the cross because He had a strong enough faith to bear it.

"That was quite a dramatic moment, the three of us in that car in that enormous empty parking lot. It made me feel better, of course, but it took a time. That night we went out for dinner with Rube Walker and his wife at the Derby Steakhouse, up past the Concourse, and I remember we had a helluva good steak, but not much conversation. It lasted for a while. Crazy people called up my family and shouted into the phone, why hadn't they taught their son how to pitch."

"And nothing now? It hasn't marked you?"

"Oh, every once in a while in a bar somebody'll say, 'Hell, there's Ralph Branca,' and some other guy will come up with a grin, 'Hey, how's Bobby Thomson?' Now what the hell am I supposed to do about that? Fall over in a faint?"

He went on to say that he felt others—not only fans, but fellow ballplayers—were far more affected by what had happened in the Polo Grounds than he was. The reverberation of the disaster resulted in a near-paranoid reaction in the Dodger organization. Branca, who wanted to wear number 13 the following spring, a number he had always been partial to, was not allowed to use it. The front office came up with all sorts of strange computations. They pointed out that the Thomson home run had been hit off him on the third day of the tenth month, which added up to thirteen, and no sir*ee*, he wasn't going to be allowed to wear *that* number. But the main thing, according to Branca, was that he was *stared* at by everyone as if they half expected him to collapse in his tracks under the weight of what he had gone through. The result was that he began to press on the mound under this sort of scrutiny, and his confidence waned. His back began to hurt him; he tried to pitch through the pain; then his arm began to give him trouble and quickly his skills suffered, never to recover. He left baseball at the age of 31 in 1957 after mediocre turns with the Detroit Tigers (where he wore number 35) and with the Yankees (where he wore number 25).

"Wherever I went I asked for 13," he told me. "But they always said no. If I had my druthers I'd still want 13. Or 44."

"Aaron's number."

"Yup. I always liked that number."

I said that I could not understand how he felt that the Thomson home run had been beneficial in any way —he had just recited a most melancholy saga.

"It was an albatross for a long time," he said. "But on the other hand I'm recognized. Why if I walked down the street with Bobby Thomson I think more people would recognize me."

I asked him why.

"Well, I think they're more interested in me," he said. "They look at me and wonder if I'm all right. I went through that terrible thing. What did it do to me? It's not that they appreciate a loser. But they're curious about how a man's difficulties affect him—it's awfully close to their own lives, and it makes them feel better to see that someone can go through that and walk around and smile and function. They want reassurances.

"And of course it's good for my business, which is with the Security Mutual Life here in Binghamton. When I pick up the phone and say, 'I'm Ralph Branca,' the person on the other end says, 'Oh?' and he'll want me to drop around and talk about baseball. That's fine with me. After a while I can get the talk shifted around to insurance. Sometimes it takes quite a while."

When we'd finished talking, I remembered sitting back and thinking what a taxing profession baseball was—never forgiving its major sinners, or forgetting them. Their reputations were stamped irrevocably with their misfortune—as if a debt to society had been incurred which could never, under any circumstances,

be absolved. Just as the Cincinnati series got under-
way, an obituary about an old ballplayer appeared in
the *New York Times* under the headline FRED SNOD-
GRASS DIES: BALLPLAYER MUFFED 1912 FLY.
The article began "Fred Carlisle Snodgrass, who muffed
an easy fly ball that helped cost the New York Giants
the 1912 World Series, died Friday at the age of 86."
Snodgrass had gone on to great things after he retired
from baseball: he was a successful banker and rancher,
the mayor of Oxnard, California—which was related in
the obituary for sure, but unrelentingly the obituary
writer came back to dwell on the indiscretion com-
mitted during the course of a second or so on a
summery afternoon some sixty years before. "Mr.
Snodgrass made a two-base muff of pinch hitter Clyde
Engle's easy [note that Snodgrass is not let off with
an unmodified "fly"—it is an "easy" chance] pop fly
to set up the tying run. One man walked and another
singled, driving in Mr. Engle to tie the game and put
the winning run on third. A long outfield fly scored
the winning run. He is survived by his widow, Jose-
phine; two daughters," etc.

The Pitcher

It always surprised me that there were not
more instances of pitchers taking it out on the batter
who had just dismayed them . . . it was easy to imagine
that in the frustration of giving up a home run the
pitcher might rush for the batter who had done it,
bellowing at him, and interrupting him on the base
paths. Bob Lemon of the Cleveland Indians once threw
his glove at Dusty Rhodes, who had hit a Chinese
home run 250 feet down the short right-field line at
the Polo Grounds in the 1954 World Series, but that
was about the extent of it. The practice is invariably
for the pitcher to take out his vengeance on the follow-

ing batter, knocking him down—as if batters were a collective menace rather than individuals.

Hank Greenberg (who told me about the Lemon episode) said that the most upset pitcher he ever saw was Wes Ferrell of the Washington Senators. He described a game in which Ferrell found himself with a 7–0 lead in the early innings. Rain began to fall, and the Detroit Tigers tried to slow down their pace, hoping that the game would be called off. The lead seemed insurmountable. Ferrell kept yelling out of his dugout that the Tigers were stalling. But in the middle innings Ferrell began to get into trouble; his lead was chipped away run by run until in the eighth the Tigers tied the game 9–9. Ferrell was taken out. He sat in his dugout, the Tigers taunting him from across the way; suddenly he began to pick his glove apart, starting on the thumb, pulling the stuffing out and dropping it on the dugout floor. When he got back to the locker room he ripped his uniform in pieces, starting at the socks, and Greenberg said that the story which went around the leagues was that at the climax of his orgy of clothes-tearing he took his watch out of his street clothes and jumped up and down on it.

Greenberg had a teammate, Fred Hutchinson, with perhaps the most famous temper of the pitchers and later of the managers. If it had been a particularly painful drubbing, Hutchinson would head down the long corridor that led out of the back of the dugout to the locker room and on the way, he would burst the row of light bulbs with his gloved hand as he strode along, every one of them, so that at the far end he would leave the tunnel pitch black; when his teammates came along later, after the game was over, they groped their way, hands feeling along the wall, their cleats crashing on the cement floor, and someone would say, "Well, ol' Hutch is sure riled. Wonder what's left of the clubhouse."

Often they would find *that* a shambles, since Hutchinson had a predilection like Ferrell's toward ripping up clothes and tipping things over until he could get his temper under control.

Jim Brosnan had some further stories about Hutchinson as a manager. He told me that Hutch always kept doing things with his fingers. That was where his rage, when he had it under control, had its outlet. They would pick at things—especially packets of chewing gum. He would open up a stick, throw the gum away, and then he'd begin working on the silver wrapper, tearing it up into tiny pieces and rolling them between his fingers into small silver balls. These fingers worked during an entire game, a rain of silver coming down whenever Hutch happened to be in the dugout. Sometimes, when the situation got tight, the fingers would leave off the gum wrappers and fetch themselves a fungo bat.

Brosnan said, "Hutch was death on fungo bats. Most teams can get through a season with three or four fungo bats, but the Detroit Tigers would order in ten or twenty because they knew that Hutch would break most of them down during the summer. He pounded them on the cement steps of the dugout. Death on fungo bats, doing that. Now most of the teams have aluminum fungo bats, which make a hell of a sound when you hit them against something—bong!—and I've often wondered how Hutch would have liked that. Probably a lot.

"When the Tigers lost, of course, he was no one to live with. His wife would hear the news on the radio, or watch it on television, and she'd turn and warn the children. One time Hutch came home after a Tiger loss —sometimes he walked miles along Michigan Avenue —and to everyone's surprise he seemed to be making an effort to keep his temper in check. He sat down for dinner with his family. He didn't say much. Then, just as he was getting up from his dessert, he turned and threw a punch in frustration, and he busted a hole in the wall right behind his chair. His wife cried out, 'Look, Hutch, what you've done!' and he growled at her, 'Hang a picture over it,' and stomped out."

Once, when I was in the Braves' camp, I heard Eddie Mathews, the Braves manager, begin talking about a Chicago pitcher named Meyer—"Mad Monk"

Meyer. On one occasion Meyer got so frustrated on the pitcher's mound when his manager came out and relieved him that he reached down and hurled the rosin bag high in the air, and trailing a slight tail of dust white it came down *puff* on his cap and he was so absorbed in disgust that he never realized it was stuck there until he got to the dugout.

"He was a strange one," said Mathews. "He carried a steamer trunk and changed his shirts four or five times a day."

Jim Brosnan also remembered the Mad Monk. Hell, they were teammates together.

"Did he look like a monk?" I asked.

"Well, it's true he had sort of chiseled features," Brosnan said. "But he certainly was no monk. I remember that game Mathews is talking about. It was the first game of a Memorial Day weekend. Adcock, Aaron, and Mathews all came up and hit home runs, Mathews's over one of those flowerpots set out in the deep stands in Wrigley Field. That was too much for the Mad Monk. He plinked Bill Bruton, the next batter, who was the Braves' center fielder, and when they took him out of there, he threw the rosin bag up in the air, just like you said, so mad he didn't notice that when it came down he was storming toward the dugout with the thing perched on the bill of his cap."

"Did he often throw tantrums?" I asked.

"Once, sitting in the john, just thinking in there, his temper suddenly got to him—I don't know what crossed his mind—and he got up and ripped the latrine door off."

"One begins to understand that name," I said.

"I don't know what's happened to him now," Brosnan continued. "He was a roaming sort, the Mad Monk. I heard he owned a bowling alley for a while, and one day he got into a big argument with the manager; he threw a bowling ball at him which went over the counter and brought down a big plate mirror that the Mad Monk was especially proud of. He liked it better than anything else in his place."

The Hitter

And what about the batters? What about their rages? Did they ever storm down that 60 feet 6 inches brandishing their bats out of sheer frustration? Charlie Gehringer once threw his bat at his own pop fly in the misbegotten hope he could knock it clear of falling into a fielder's glove.

Most of them seemed to take it out on the water coolers, but there were exceptions. Norman Cash once got so frustrated at Nolan Ryan's pitching that he brought a *table leg* up to the batter's box—somebody had sent it to him in the mail—an odd gesture, really, since it indicated his tortured state of mind. Indeed, Ryan, perhaps bolstered by this gesture toward his invincibility, went on in that game to pitch a no-hitter.

Then there were the more serious actions—the sort of furious duels like the Carl Furillo–Sal Maglie match-ups in which often Furillo pushed a bunt down the first-base line in the hope of trampling over Maglie on his way down the base path. Jackie Robinson tried this maneuver once, barreling into the man covering first base, who turned out not to be Maglie but Davey Williams, the Giant second baseman, who reinjured his back in the crack-up and was finished in baseball.

The strangest manifestation of the rivalry between pitcher and batter was provided me by Jim Bouton, former Yankee pitcher and the author of *Ball Four*—about an outfielder named Fred Loesekam, who played in the Chicago White Sox farm system for an obscure team called the Holdredge (Nebraska) White Sox. He *hated* the opposing teams, especially the pitchers, so much so that he became known for his habit during pre-game practice of lobbing high flies into the midst of the opposition, especially the pitchers. If he saw a clutch of pitchers standing around gossiping, or getting ready to run laps in the outfield, he'd peg a long high shot at them, and then he'd move a few yards and try it again.

"He was very hard to catch at this," Bouton said. "He'd toss the ball so high that it was up there in the sky like a mortar shell, and as it came down he'd cross his arms and casually look the other way. It'd land *thump,* right among us, and everybody'd look around—I mean the thing could have come over the outfield wall—it just *materialized,* whistling down, *bang.* Finally, one day he was caught at it. Well, that was it. The pitchers drew a target map of him—like what you find in a butcher's shop with the portions divided *rump steak, top sirloin, ground chuck,* and so forth, and we hung it up in the locker room. Some areas of Mr. Loesekam were more valuable than the others—sort of like Pin the Tail on the Outfielder. Hitting him in the foot was worth hardly anything at all. You can imagine what area was priced the highest."

"Were you serious about all this?" I asked.

"We never got him," Bouton went on. "We worked on him all summer like there was a bounty on his head. We wanted to get him so bad, but we kept missing him. Of course, the umpires only'd give you a few shots—I mean you can't throw at will at a man's body."

"How did he take to this?" I asked.

Bouton laughed. "He was a big fellow, six two, and fast. He dug right in, but you could see he was prepared to move quickly. The closest I ever got to him was when I threw the ball just where you're supposed to if you want to deck a man: right behind his head, which instinctively he'll back into. Well, I did that, fired the ball behind his head, and he froze. Absolutely. The ball hit his bat cocked back on his shoulder and bounced out to the pitcher's mound and I threw him out. What I remember most is that he never came out of the batter's box to run for first base. He was just stunned."

There is nothing at all like this sort of confrontation in sports—that I can think of, at any rate—in which two people face each other in a match-up involving two entirely different skills. The measure of baseball is that it works at all, and that one department does not overwhelm the other. A balance between pitcher and batter remains reasonable and constant however furious the duel between the two—and that was why when one achieved superiority over the other it was momentary and thus to be relished all the more . . . such as the way Pete Rose circled the bases in the 1972 World Series on his home run, never taking his eyes off the pitcher, Catfish Hunter of the Oakland A's, except to make sure he touched the bases, his mouth ajar, sneering his disdain.

Even when the pitcher's mound and the batter's box were deserted there seemed to be an invisible quiet current between them, and I always half expected, walking across the infield after a game, to detect a faint hum from the lane like the thin metallic whine that drifts off high-voltage wires . . . so that one was tempted to go around behind home plate rather than cut across. It was like crossing a railroad track in the country—the sense of turbulence just past, and the stillness poised for interruption once again.

The Observer

This morning in the hotel lobby I happened to run into Neil Leiffer, a *Sports Illustrated* photographer. On opening day he had found himself coming down in the elevator with the black police lieutenant who had arrested the streaker who had been capering about in the top tier of Riverfront. The lieutenant was very agitated—perhaps more puzzled than furious. He had been roundly booed for what he undoubtedly referred to newsmen later in officialese as "apprehending the perpetrator . . ." and it rankled him to think (as he put it to the people in the elevator) "that I was doing my duty and I was being booed and this guy was *signing autographs* on his way to the pokey."

When I got back to my room I tried calling up the

streaker, out of curiosity, and wondering what he would remember about it all. His name was in the *Cincinnati Enquirer* and I looked up his number in the Dayton directory. He came on the phone with a soft, faintly timid voice, full of "Yes, sirs," and at first I suspected that he would shy away from discussing what he had done. Not at all. He carried me through his day of streaking if not with relish, certainly with little prompting. In the background I could occasionally hear someone saying "Oh, Mark!" (his name was Mark Koors), a voice he later identified as belonging to his mother. She had been mortified by the whole episode.

He described how he and twelve others had motored down to Cincinnati on the morning of April 4. Most of them were friends from his days at Chaminade High School, and for four years the group had regularly been attending opening day. It had become a tradition for them. They had lunch in the Stadium Club. Mark had quite a few beers and a couple of sips of blackberry wine which he didn't much care for, and he decided to stick to the beer. The group was in its seats at the top of the third tier for the Aaron home run in the first inning. All of them expected it—at lunch someone had pointed out that Aaron had hit more home runs off Reds' pitching than any other staff in the league—but when it happened they could hardly believe it. They talked about what a "great deal" it was to have been there—"to see history made."

In the sixth inning Mark and a friend of his named Tim went down and stood in line to get some beer. Someone in the line said that he was surprised that no one had tried streaking the stadium.

"Was it Tim who said that?" I asked.

"Sir?"

"Was it Tim . . . ?"

"No sir. But Tim looked at me and said, 'Why don't *you* do it?' It wasn't a dare, really. It was just a sort of suggestion. It seemed interesting to me. So right there in the beer line I began to take off my clothes. I was wearing a light jacket, a gold-colored shirt, a green and white plaid pair of double-knit trousers, and a pair of oxblood shoes. I had got down to my undershorts, which were white, when this policeman came walking over. He asked, 'What are you doing?'

"I said, 'Who, me? Nothing.'

"He told me to put my clothes back on in a hurry. He stood there while I did. He told me that there wasn't going to be that sort of thing, not in his area. But then he went wandering off. By this time the thought was in my mind. I said to Tim, 'I think I'll just go ahead and streak this place.' "

"Oh, Mark!" I could hear the voice in the background.

"So we went to the men's room. There were some people standing around washing their hands while I took off my clothes. Tim sang that funky honky-tonk stripping song—the one with the big beat. The people looked sort of surprised. I handed my clothes to Tim and walked out the door and past the beer line. Some of the others in our group had come down and were standing there. I yelled at them and they turned and began laughing. I tried to run back up to my seat, but the aisles were clogged with people and they would turn around and yell. Some people shielded their eyes. There was a lot of cheering, and then I got to my seat and put on my clothes; people leaned over and congratulated me and said that it was a good idea to streak Riverfront Stadium. But there were other people up there who began pointing and soon enough about five policemen arrived, including the one who had seen me in the beer line. 'I told you not to do it,' he said.

"They took me down the aisle. On the way I signed some autographs and a kid stuck out a baseball which I signed. They took me to the police station. My friends came by after the game and bailed me out for fifty dollars. At the time I thought it was kind of fun. Of course, I was drinking beer. The only bad part was getting caught; I could have done without that.

"Sir? Well, my feeling was that history was made twice that day—Aaron's home run, and baseball's first streaker. The foreman at the printshop where I work showed me this news clipping which recommended that the clothes I wore that day be put in the Hall of Fame at Cooperstown."

"Oh, Mark!"

"Sir? Oh, it might be the last time I streak. Perhaps not. If the right occasion came up where some place *needed* streaking . . . I thought it would be kind of funny if I went down and streaked the game in Atlanta."

"Oh, Mark!"

"Now that I've done it, I think about places which ought to be streaked. The Dayton Mall, for example. They have a deputy sheriff out in the parking lot. Have to watch out for him. A lot of people want me to streak again. One girl said it was immature; but others thought it was pretty funny.

"Was it sensual? Not *that* day, no sir. I got no sexual thing out of it at all. I was a little too drunk. If I ever do it again . . ."

"Mark!"

"Sir? That's my mother. She's sitting over there having a fit. She wants to forget the whole business. You'd like to talk to her?"

His mother came on the phone with a soft, emotional voice, very much like her son's.

"His friends dared him. He had too much beer. It was the combination of that, and the opening game, and the nicest sort of weather, and the Aaron home run . . . and I was just devastated. The police called to verify that it was him. He didn't have his billfold. I told him not to take it because I thought he might lose it, so he was without any identification. They called me and said they had arrested him for public indecency. 'Not *my* son,' I told them. Oh, it was mortifying."

"Oh, ma." I could hear his thin voice in the background.

"We didn't go down and bail him out. His father is an invalid and we knew he was there with friends. It was so upsetting. The trouble is that he's so darn *big*. He's six one or two and he lifts weights, so he's very hard to miss unless he's sitting down. I wished he was small so nobody could have seen him. But boy, oh boy! The whole family was very upset. The worst thing was that the paper got his name wrong here in Dayton. The Cincinnati paper had it right. His full name is Mark

Robert Koors, but the Dayton paper left off the Mark.
He has a cousin, Robert Koors, just back from the
service in Germany, practically just off the *boat,* and
boy oh boy did he ever walk into it—phone calls, and
friends yelling at him in the street, and he didn't know
what had *happened*. What a nightmare for poor Robert.
He just got the *heck* for it all. How silly it all was. I
just couldn't believe it."

"Oh, ma."

The Hitter

Aaron had a rotten game that Sunday—
striking out against Clay Kirby on three straight pitches
the first two times he was at bat, and in the field in-
explicably backing up to let a playable fly ball by Perez
drop in front of him. Mathews removed him in the
seventh inning, not as a punitive measure, obviously,
but because he had by then fulfilled the commissioner's
edict; substituting a more mobile defensive man (usually
Ralph Garr) for Aaron in the late innings was a common enough maneuver for the Braves. The Braves'
people were probably terribly relieved, except for
Aaron, of course. He couldn't have liked it at all. He
was questioned by Dick Young for not playing to his
utmost. Almost as a therapeutic measure Aaron began
thinking about Al Downing, the Los Angeles pitcher
scheduled to pitch on Monday night in Atlanta. He
thought about him most of the way down on the plane
. . . thinking about his fast ball which tails away and
which if he's right is his best pitch. He knew that
Downing wouldn't want to throw him curve balls,
which from a left-hander would come inside, and which
he could pull. He began to set himself mentally for the
one pitch he could rely on seeing—the Downing fast
ball. He knew it would come sooner or later. . . .

The Observer

On the way down in the plane to Atlanta I finished reading a first-rate book about the Indianapolis Clowns entitled *Some Are Called Clowns*. Henry Aaron had played a few weeks with them in 1951, and then was offered two hundred a month to play with them the following year. A month and a half into that season, John Mullen, the Braves' farm director, sent one of his scouts, Dewey Griggs, to look at the young infielder (he was playing shortstop then). Griggs happened in on a doubleheader in Buffalo in which Aaron got seven hits out of nine, two of them home runs. He sent such an enthusiastic report to the home office that the Braves offered an option to purchase Aaron's contract for $10,000 . . . which naturally was the end of Aaron's career with the Clowns.

But what an extraordinary institution he had been involved in! The Clowns, the last of the barnstorming teams, were originally an all-black team which had its origins in the Negro leagues and integrated in reverse in 1968. The team had been on the road for over forty consecutive seasons. Aaron was, of course, its most illustrious graduate. Other ex-Clowns include Choo-Choo Coleman, the first Met to hit a home run, Paul Casanova, originally from Cuba, who is now with the Braves, and George Smith, once with the Red Sox and now out of baseball. The great track star Jesse Owens traveled with the Clowns for a season, just after his victory in the 1936 Olympic Games in Berlin. He was featured in a horse race after the game was over—a 60-yard sprint which he invariably won because the *bang* of the starter's pistol caused the horse to rear, which gave Owens a big jump.

Satchel Paige played for the Clowns when he was about 60 years old. The procedure, since he was a hard man to keep track of and kept disappearing and being left behind when the team bus drove out of town, was to get him into his uniform as soon as possible after pulling into a town and then get him out on the nearest stream with his fishing rod and bait. That was his special love, and the small boys would come along the riverbank and see the old man in his baseball uniform looking at the red-painted bob floating on the water. After infield practice someone would be sent to fetch him, and he would arrive at the beginning of the game still able, in the inning or so he pitched, to get the opposition out. He threw pitches he referred to as "dipsy-doodles."

The trademark of the Clowns was entertainment—much like a low-grade baseball counterpart to the clowning activities of the Harlem Globetrotters. For years the team included a midget (who played third base), a juggler who did ball-handling feats, and once a contortionist (called the Great Yogi) who stood on one hand in the first-base coach's box to disconcert the opposing pitcher. ("He'd stand on one hand there, his arm and two legs tangled up so it looked like they had to be broken. Then he'd sort of—*move* them in this special way he had. Women used to scream and all. Great attraction.") One of their great pitching acts was a man called Double Duty Green who was ambidextrous and could fling fast balls from either side. He wore a special glove which fit both hands.

Many of the Clowns' routines involved firecrackers. A cherry bomb would go off behind the ump, and send the batter skittering in fright down the baseline to jump in the third-base coach's arms. The first baseman, a player called Nature Boy Williams, a sturdy, heavy-set fellow who often dressed in women's clothes to play, would occasionally put a torpedo in his first baseman's mitt which would go off if the throw was hard, and the smoke would pour out of the glove.

Many of the routines had a somewhat raunchy flavor. In Newport News, the mayor was upset by a gag in which the lady umpire (the wife of the team's factotum general manager) goosed one of the ballplayers when he was standing in the batter's box. The mayor canceled their booking for the following year.

It was a good book to read—warm with the empathy that comes so easily in following the adventures of a band traveling in a ramshackle bus through the small backwoods communities of the country for the one-stop games against home teams with names like Dick's Supermarket Home Talent, Fargo Glass & Paint, Rippy Auto Parts. I envied the author, a young writer named William Heward, with an excellent ear, a wonderfully idiomatic style, peppy and original, drawing from a year (1972) which he spent pitching for the Clowns, perhaps the last year of their existence. Someone said today that they had just gone out of business.

One passage caught my eye:

We were scheduled in New Ellington, a little town of five hundred in South Carolina. We dressed in groups of three in a broken-down outhouse behind third base. This "dressing room" was also a warehouse for a shattered sink, umpire paraphernalia, and the Coca-Cola and hot dog buns for the concession stand. Zucchi [a pitcher who had just arrived from a small Wisconsin town], sitting on cases of pop, flicked a daddy-longlegs off his calf and said, "I don't like this, I don't have to like this, and I'm going home."

New Ellington is black and very poor, but they give you the best they've got. (They also gave us a mean 6-foot 6-inch hard-throwing left-hander who beat us 3–2.) Three hundred people showed up for the game and stood along the foul lines. There are only seats for about fifty. We've played cities of fifty thousand and not drawn three hundred. Both the temperature and the humidity were well into the nineties, and we were dead tired from an all-night jump. Yet you wanted to play your heart out. The people seemed to be enjoying it so much, and it was obvious there's not much chance for laughter in New Ellington. After the game we were invited in twos and threes to some of the townspeople's houses for a shower and a snack. In a tin-roofed shack that stood on wooden legs Zucchi and I sat and ate fried chicken, corn bread, and collard greens until we were bloated.

Aaron would not have shared Zucchi's feelings. I had talked about the Clowns with him for just a moment in the locker room last year. He seemed to have considerable nostalgia for those early days of his career—perhaps because the press of reporters was building up around his cubicle, and he knew he had a winter of the pressure of the home runs ahead of him. The Clowns were apparently not as fun-loving when Aaron was with them. He told me that the team had a dwarf with them—Little Bebob, who was a sort of clown—and he would sneak up and pour dirt into players' shoes, and he set off a firecracker once in a while. But he was on the team to aggravate the opposition; he didn't play.

"The only clowning around we did," Aaron said, "was a shadowball show—pretending to throw the ball around the infield—which we did before the game started. Then it was down to business. We were a fine team. We traveled in a bus, all jammed up so some of us had to sit on the floor. I wouldn't care for it much now. But then. Oh my! I wasn't yet 20 and they called me Little Brother and it was like the major leagues . . ."

The Observer

Well, here we are in Atlanta. The road show has moved. And damned if there are not tornado warnings. From the hotel window I've just seen a rain squall thrash across the roofs below; it rolled a children's scooter across a lawn and toppled it over against a fence. But the weather is clearing and the game tonight is scheduled. The radio console by the bed has been hammering the ears with a pair of Henry Aaron songs. One of them, author and composer unknown, goes:

> Hammerin' Henry,
> You're number one now.
> Henry, we're so proud of you,
> Henry, your bat rang true.

Before the game in Atlanta, Aaron is escorted onto the field by Braves announcer Milo Hamilton.

On deck for the second time.

The swing that broke the record.

Photos by Bud Skin

Pitcher Al Downing follows the flight of the ball.

Aaron approaches home and a large welcoming committee.

Jubilation.

Sports Illustrated photo by Herb Scharfman © Time, Inc.

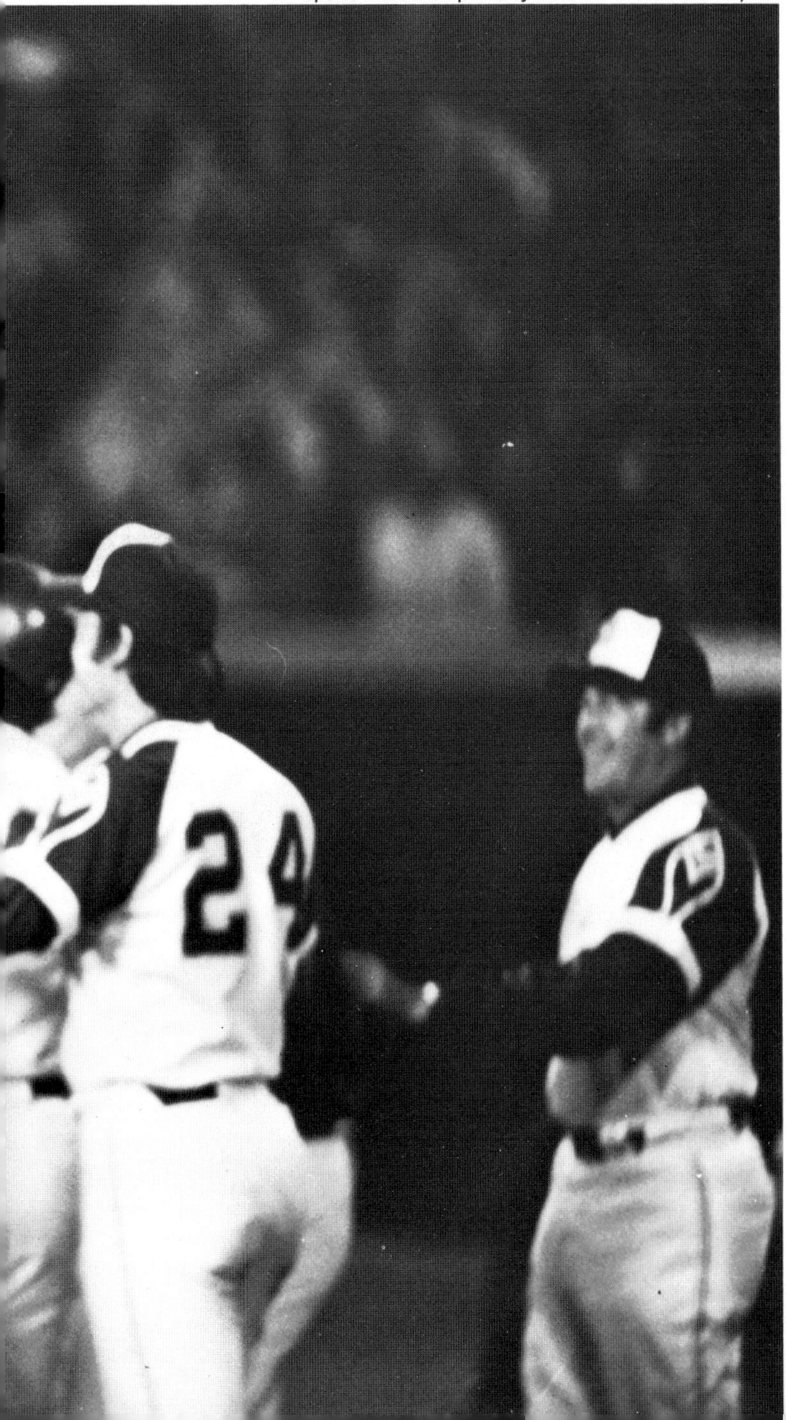

The ball and the new champion who hit it.

The other is by the former Pittsburgh Pirates pitcher Nelson Briles, one of the more musical players in the leagues, who was once invited to sing the national anthem—which he did with enough competence so that clubhouse wits around the league last year referred to him as the only Pittsburgh pitcher who could finish anything. He is also known for a pitching style which often ends up with his falling down in a heap at the follow-through of his delivery—his record being 13 tumbles in one game. His song is entitled "Hey, Hank, I Know You're Goin' t'Do It But Please Don't Hit It Off Me"—the authenticity of his feelings somewhat dimmed by the fact that during the winter he was traded to Kansas City in the American League and could no longer possibly face Aaron in a situation involving the 715th home run.

One of his verses goes as follows:

> Please!
> I've gotta reputation
> And I've gotta fam-il-y
> So please don't hit it
> So please don't hit it
> So please don't hit it off of me.

Between these songs the disk jockey has been having a lot of fun at the expense of the baseball commissioner. The latter is obviously not popular here because of his "tampering" (as an Atlanta fan would describe it) with the Braves' lineup in Cincinnati. The word had come through that the commissioner would not be attending the game that night. He was sending Monte Irvin, the ex-Giant third baseman now working in the commissioner's office, as his deputy—the reason given being that the commissioner was scheduled to address a dinner in Cleveland.

"So here we are," the radio announcer said, "with the most important moment in baseball history, perhaps in *athletic* history, and the commissioner is having dinner in *Cleve*land—" his voice turgid with scorn. "Now I have no ill respect to the city of *Cleve*land," he continued, "but no dinner in *Cleve*land is worth this game and that I feel duty bound to say!"

A dramatic pause.

"And now (the radio announcer's voice continues) a true goldie for today . . . 'Hammerin' Henry' ":

> Henry, we're so proud of you,
> Henry, your bat rang true.

The hotel is full of funeral directors—a convention of them, wearing their name tags under plastic covers on their lapels. What on earth do they talk about in the suites set aside for their meetings? All of those I saw were black—ample, cheerful men in the elevators, always wearing ties, and I was never able to catch their eye for a morning greeting.

I wondered if it was because they were black, or funeral directors, and decided it was the latter, that even a friendly acknowledgment by a funeral director in an elevator has the suggestion of being "measured." The whole business has been on my mind. A news-magazine this morning described an Atlanta mortician, a man named Hershel Thornton (I wondered if I'd been in his company in the hotel elevator), who as a service to his "clients" (was that the right word?) at no extra cost was delighted to prop up the deceased in his open coffin by one of the bay windows on a U-shaped driveway, set up at a slant, so that friends and relatives could cruise by and pay their last respects without ever getting out of their cars.

This morning almost every person I saw in the hotel (funeral directors included) was wearing a paper cow-boy hat with an orange cardboard sunburst in front that reads 715. The whole town is humming . . . which breeds this odd sense of the inevitable. It reminds me of Atlanta on the night of the Quarry-Ali fight some years ago—the same *frisson* of anticipation. But how strange to think of this in terms of a *baseball* game, and the assurance that their man is going to hit a home run for them . . . an impossibly difficult feat . . . after all how many times at bat did Aaron come up before he could be considered due to hit a home run? What happens if he hits four pop-ups tonight? What do people do with those cowboy hats, these souvenirs of a vast nonhappening? And imagine the strain on Aaron. And Downing, the pitcher, just about to be dropped on the spinning roulette wheel, what must this do to him, stepping off the plane early this morning (the Dodgers got in at one thirty this morning, I hear) into this atmosphere of expectation? Do you suppose the clerks, half dazed with sleep behind the counter, looked up and said to themselves, Well there he is . . . poor guy . . .

The Fan

A packed stadium is apparently assured for tonight. The baby blue seats will be completely covered . . . a welcome and very rare sight for the Braves' management. On the road the attendance figures are up over a million—with an average of 5,000 more people a game turning up than at home. Atlanta has severe attendance problems and no one is quite sure why, or what to do about it, short of producing a pennant contender.

Nowhere was the situation more evident than in the special VIP box constructed near the Braves' dugout where the commissioner of baseball, Bowie Kuhn, sat in lordly solitude for the last games of the 1973 season until the Braves' management scurried around and "papered the box" with a number of startled fans moved down from their seats to cluster around the commissioner in case a photographer or television camera happened to point in that direction.

No one understands why this situation exists in Atlanta. The ball park is within walking distance of downtown, an architectural pleasure with ample parking, and there is an interesting team of sluggers besides Aaron which *should* draw customers. But the Braves contend with a near-quixotic attitude on the part of the community.

The advance sales are invariably slight; but sometimes, suddenly, as many as 40,000 tickets to a single
game have been sold at the gate—as if that enormous
segment of the population of Atlanta had suddenly
pushed back their chairs from the lunch table and collectively decided to spend the afternoon at the ball
park. The management, at a loss to plot these cycles,
blames its problem on any number of factors—the
quick spring and summer rains, a club that has wal-
lowed at the bottom of the league despite its clutch of
home-run hitters, a fear of being mugged (the well-
known Atlanta sports columnist Jesse Outlar was shot
and nearly killed after a Falcon game by a man in the
stadium parking lot who thought he was carrying the
gate receipts in an attaché case), and especially the
curious disinterest of the blacks, who make up the
largest middle-class black community in the country.

In 1973 the major leagues hired the Lieberman Research Corporation to do a survey on baseball entitled
*How Sports Fans Feel About Baseball—an Attitudinal
and Motivational Investigation.* It cost $160,000. It
is an enormous loose-leaf compilation of charts and
polls which sits on the top shelf of every public-rela-
tions office in the league—most of which repeats the
same information in different forms. The survey's
people had interviewed 3,776 sports fans to reach their
conclusions. One chart that intrigued me was titled
"Images of Major League Baseball."

Most of the responses were quite predictable: 64
percent, the highest percentage, think of baseball as a
"good warm weather sport"; 63 percent, "a truly American sport"; 62 percent, "a game that's good for the
whole family"; 54 percent, "it's fun to watch in person"; 53 percent, "it requires great team play"; 44 percent, "it requires great skill" (the one I would have
voted for)—down on through "good value for the
money" . . . 28 percent; a "game that helps me forget
my troubles" . . . 19 percent; and "a game that calms
me down" . . . 13 percent. At the bottom of the poll
were two surprising findings. Five percent of the people
interviewed thought that baseball was "a good *indoor*
game," and 4 percent, a "good *cold weather* sport."

How odd. Who were *these* interviewees—the 180-odd people who picked these strange categories for what they considered their "image" of baseball?

The fans were fairly rough on the Braves. After Aaron, who was, of course, their favorite player, the next Brave listed was Ralph Garr, at number five and following Willie Mays, Johnny Bench, and Pete Rose. The fans gave their team below-average ratings in terms of a number of categories: *excitement, teamwork among players, colorful players, talented players, community-minded players, community identification with team.*

A number of the report's suggestions caught my eye —"home-run hitting contests"; "female ushers and attendants"; "drawings for free tickets to future games"; that "rock idols" participate in a two-inning pregame contest; that "ethnic players" be used in promotional activities to try to get the "ethnic fans to come on out": that the TV cameras zoom in and "pick out blacks and other ethnic fans as well as white fans." Henry Aaron, of course, was seen as the key figure in the analysis of the Braves—but it was firmly pointed out that his image should be that of a team member, not of a star around which the team had been built. To promote this concept it was suggested that the Braves have a "pepper game" (presumably with Aaron involved) as part of the pregame warm-ups to point out how well the players "work together."

According to the report blacks are not oriented to outdoor events as much as whites (were they the ones whose wishful thinking produced the image of baseball being a "good indoor game"?). The report says that blacks prefer to go to (in order) (1) movies, (2) amusement parks, and (3) nightclubs. The whites' preferences are (1) restaurants, (2) play participation, (3) camping. Baseball, or sports viewing in general, is not mentioned in this breakdown—so it is difficult to understand the rationale . . . that people who prefer to eat out, play softball, and go on hikes are more enthusiastic about baseball than those who like to take in a film, ride the Ferris wheel, and go out on the town at night. More pertinent is the observation that whites seem to concern themselves with the traditional aspects of baseball—statistics, history . . . both categories combined in the sort of "chase" that Aaron was making for Babe Ruth's record.

Aaron himself felt that the problem with the blacks was simply the adversity of their situation. It had been the same in Milwaukee when the club was there. The park had not received its share of blacks there, either. It was probably because they were tired after the hard day of working, and the children, and the feeding of their families, and the general difficulty of life, and it wasn't so easy to put down the dollars to come out to the ballpark.

The Hitter

conversation in a cab

"So you're just sticking around until he hits it. Is it going to be quick?"

"Maybe tonight. Everybody seems to think so. Even the writers. There were some people that came ready for a long siege—big suitcases, and scared that he might flounder around for a month or so. But not now."

"Who's pitching for the other club?"

"Al Downing," I told him. "A left-hander, which will be to Aaron's advantage."

"Does Aaron name his bats? The Brown Bomber?"

"No, you're thinking of Joe Louis. Or Black Betsy, which was Babe Ruth's bat. He's very matter-of-fact about his equipment. For play on artificial surfaces he wears an old pair of plastic-bottomed shoes that Joe Pepitone left behind him when he shipped out to play baseball in Japan. He has no particular fussiness about his bats. Orlando Cepeda . . . he had as many as twenty cluttering up the bat rack. But Aaron, he sticks with a bat once he likes it and has only one spare on hand in case he (or worse, a pitcher who picks it up for batting practice) cracks it. . . ."

"What do you know that's surprising about him?"

"Well, I'm not sure he likes to hit home runs very much."

"Oh, come on!"

"When you visit a clubhouse after a game, you can always tell who's hit a home run, almost by the way he sits on the stool in front of his locker. He just *exudes* the sense of having done something pretty grand. He can hardly wait to talk to someone about it. But not Aaron. Home runs are rather down the scale, that's what I mean, of the things he likes. He'd rather talk about what he *used* to do and no longer can to such a degree—about his base stealing, for example. He stole 31 bases in one year with that sort of gliding deceptive way that was never terribly exciting to watch but was like Joe DiMaggio's—effective and always done at just the right time so it meant something in the outcome of the game. He may be prouder of his record of getting over 3,000 hits. I know he thinks of Ty Cobb's record of 4,191 as being the most remarkable—not the Ruth record."

"Is he blasé about baseball?"

"He never winds down. All year. He told me he sees the pitchers in his dreams and he jumps."

"Is that the most extraordinary record—Cobb's?"

"I have a friend in Philadelphia who's on the paper there—Larry Swindell of the *Inquirer*—who is a trivia expert of sorts and he just snorts when he thinks of that Cobb record. He says that the great one is Sam Crawford's record of 312 triples, which no one has approached. It's never going to be beaten because triples are so hard to come by these days."

"So Aaron doesn't take particular pride in his home runs?"

"Well, after the opener in Cincinnati I went up to him and said, 'Hey, that was great—the 714th home run!'—with this big smile . . . but he was affected by

the fact that the Braves had lost that game. They had
the champagne ready for him, and they would have
put it out on the tables if he'd given them the go-ahead
to celebrate. But he told them to put it away."

"The Braves had better win the night he hits 715."

"That's right! He's likely to postpone the celebration
until he gets a match-up of home run and a Braves win.
He's said about home runs that if the team is behind
2–1 in the eighth, he goes for it. If they're ahead 8–1,
he also goes for it. Otherwise, he says he does what he
can to help with the game. 'First you play baseball;
then you play to win; then you try for home runs.'
That's a quote of his."

"I wonder if Ruth felt something like that?"

"Oh, I think he showed his joy. I remember a description Hank Greenberg gave me of Ruth. He was
just a rookie then with the Detroit Tigers and Ruth,
of course, was at the end of his career. Greenberg referred to him as a big Santa Claus. He always came out
onto the field last. Everybody'd yell at him, 'How you
feeling, Babe?' and he'd answer, 'Pussy good, pussy
good.' That was his favorite expression. There was
always a guy hanging round to fetch him his bicarbon-
ate and soda. He'd call out, 'Bicarb, boy!' He was gar-
gantuan in every respect. A big ham. No one resented
it. When he swung at the ball he knocked all the air
out of the park. Greenberg said that no first baseman
ever played close to the bag when the Babe was at bat;
he just backed up on the grass, even if there was a
base runner. No one ever hit pop-ups like he did; . . .
no one in the infield ever wanted to catch those enormous high things which never seemed to come down.

"But Aaron—I'll tell you something else he says—
he doesn't even watch his home runs go into the
stands."

"No kidding!"

"Some baseball people dispute that—you can see his
head turned. But he's very positive about it. So maybe
he blocks it out. Maybe it's too quick—that trot around
the bases—and what he'd really like to do is get on
with a single so he could continue that confrontation

with the pitcher—the "guessing game" which he says is the best thing in baseball. A home run closes it out, like picking up the deck of cards off the table and putting it in your pocket."

The Pitcher

Al Downing had realized during the Cincinnati series that he was to pitch the opener in Atlanta, that he would be providing the model for Thomas Wolfe's grand description: ". . . the pitcher who stands out there all alone, calm, desperate, and forsaken in his isolation." The notion did not bother Downing overly. Now a veteran of long service, he is not an overpowering pitcher, but he has great confidence, relying on perfect control and a good change of pace.

Watching him pitch in his early days with the New York Yankees a lot of people were reminded of Whitey Ford—"Blackie Ford," the press sometimes called him. He had an easy motion out of which flashed a tremendous whippy fast ball and he led the league in strikeouts in 1964. Then, throwing a curve ball to Andy Etchebarren of the Baltimore Orioles, something popped in his arm, and at the age of 27 he sagged back into the New York farm system to try to get his arm in shape. He was finally traded to Oakland, then Milwaukee, who traded him to the Los Angeles Dodgers for a player named Andy Kosco. With the Dodgers he found his form, a different kind of pitcher, but a very effective one. His teammates call him "Ace"—an encomium for winning 20 games in 1971. He is also called "Gentleman Al" for his bearing not only off the field but around the mound where he behaves, as Vince Scully, the Los Angeles announcer, has pointed out, "like a man wearing a bowler hat." He is very much his own boss, shaking off his catcher's signs as many as

25 pitches a game, and relying on his own concepts, and always on his sense that much of pitching is "feel." ("If you don't 'feel' you can throw a curve at a particular time, there's not much point in trying.") He is such a student of his craft that he always made it a point to room with a hitter, rare in a society in which there is such a confrontation between the two specialists.

We got talking about it in the locker room before the game. He said, "It helps a pitcher to be exposed to the enemy camp. For years I roomed with Maury Wills and it helped my pitching considerably just listening to him talk about hitting. At the very best I knew if I ever had to pitch to him—if either of us was traded away—that I knew something of his thought process as a batter and might be able to take advantage of it.

"Aaron? Well, I'm not sure that rooming with him for ten years would really help. You can have all the know-how, but if you make one small mistake there's no one in the league who can take advantage of it like he does. He knows what I can throw. He hit two home runs off me last year. But I'm not going to change my pattern. I mustn't go against what I've been successful with . . . I shouldn't rearrange pitches that complement each other."

"You mean you'd never try to fool him with something different?" I asked.

"Well, sometimes you throw a pitch just in the hope of getting some idea of what the hitter is thinking . . . like an off-speed pitch out of the strike zone . . . just to see how he reacts. By the way the batter anticipates, the pitcher can tell if he's looking for a fast ball—he'll be way out in front of it. And that tells the pitcher something, and he can go on from there. Of course, sometimes the batter will purposefully fool you, 'decoy' you, we call it. Willie Mays was very good at this. He'd look completely fooled by an off-speed pitch, practically fall *down* he'd be so far out in front; so the pitcher'd think, 'Well, now, maybe I can throw him another.' But this time Mays, who was praying he'd fooled the pitcher into doing it, well, his face'd light up to see that ball drifting up to him, and he'd time it right and spank it out of there. Mays was very good at that.

"My theory is that you *have* to go with what the best is that you have. Aaron knows what I know. He knows what I'd *like* to throw to him, and perhaps he'll dig in and wait for it. Now I can change speeds and move the ball around, but both he and I know that the sinking ball, low and outside, is what is going to give him the most trouble. I cannot throw that out of the arsenal because he expects it of me. I'm going to challenge him with it."

I had no idea, of course, what Aaron was going to decide to wait on, what sort of pitch his mind would lock on to the exclusion of all else—but I recall, watching Downing sitting on his stool pulling on his long socks, that I had a strong feeling of presentiment . . . that anyone, however professional, with such a straightforward approach to facing Aaron—*challenging* his disciplines with a pitch that Aaron would expect of him . . . well, that such a course was doom-ridden.

Some pitchers had come up with extreme notions of how to pitch to Aaron. Sal Maglie, who was a pitcher of blazing malevolence, had said, "The only way I could handle Aaron was to get his face in the dirt. Then he'd be edgy and I could work on him. Not always, but sometimes. It was the only way I could pitch to him."

Downing, of course, didn't have the disposition of a Maglie. He was going to meet Aaron on his own terms, and I was reminded of the latter's confident dictum that he felt he ultimately had the advantage over the pitcher. "I've got a bat, and all *he's* got is a ball. I figure that gives me the edge."

So I asked Downing if he had any superstitions.

"Six runs," he said. "Six runs in the first inning." The gap between his two front teeth showed as he grinned. "That's the best one. Look," he said more seriously, "if I throw 715 I'm not going to run and hide. There's no disgrace in that. On the other hand I'm not going to run into the plate to congratulate him. It's a big home run for him, for the game, for the country, but not for me!"

The Retriever

There was hardly a fan who turned up in the Atlanta Stadium left-field seats that night who did not firmly believe that he was going to catch the Aaron home run. Many of them brought baseball gloves. A young Atlantan from the Highway Department had established himself in the front row wielding a 15-feet-long bamboo pole with a fishnet attached. He was proficient with it, sweeping it back and forth over the Braves' bullpen. He had started coming to the ball park the previous season. He told me that at home his stepsister tossed up baseballs over the winter for him to practice on. The closest he had come to catching anything in the ball park with his gear had been a batting-practice home run hit into the bullpen enclosure the year before by a catcher named Freddie Valasquez. He missed sweeping it in by a couple of feet.

The left-field stands of Atlanta Stadium contain the cheapest seats in the ball park and perhaps its more knowledgeable and intractable fans. They have a close affinity with Aaron. He stands immediately in front of them when the Braves are in the field, and they look down at the big red-trimmed blue 44 on the back of his uniform and watch the way he rests his oversized glove ("These days I need all the glove I can get") on his hip between pitches. They rise and cheer him when he walks out to his position, and he lifts his throwing hand in an awkward, shy gesture to acknowledge them.

The Braves' outfield is bordered by a high wire-mesh fence which runs around the perimeter of the grass. In the space between it and the high wall of the stands are the two bullpens. The visitors' bullpen is in the right-field corner. The Braves' mascot, Chief Nok-A-Homa, sits in his tepee on the left-field foul line, adjacent to the Atlanta bullpen, and when a Braves' batter hits a home run he steps out in his regalia and does a war dance. The Braves' bullpen is immediately under the left-field wall; the fans with front-row seats can look down and see the catchers resting their right knees on towels to keep their pants legs from getting dusty as they warm up the relief pitchers.

The Braves' bullpen array was the weakest in either league last year (the reason that the Braves, despite a Murderers' Row of Darrell Evans, Aaron, Dusty Baker, Mike Lum, and Dave Johnson, who last year broke Rogers Hornsby's home-run record for second basemen, were not pennant contenders), and the left-field fans have the same sort of despairing affection for the relievers that Mets fans had for their team in its early bleak days. "We *know* the pitchers out here," one fan told me. "In the expensive part of the stadium they never see them long enough to get acquainted. They go in and they're bombed and they're on their way to the showers which are kept going full and heavy. They never turn off the showers once the starting pitcher is knocked out."

The main reason, of course, for sitting in the left-field corner is that the majority of Aaron's home runs are pulled toward there, either to reach the stands, or to land in the enclosure where a denizen of the bullpen or Chief Nok-A-Homa will retrieve it. Nok-A-Homa says he has seen every home run Aaron has hit in Atlanta Stadium since 1969 with the exception of number 698, which he missed because he was trying to find a chair for one of the bullpen pitchers. He has not retrieved an Aaron home run since 671, being too busy doing his celebratory foot-stomping dance, but being brisk of foot himself and outfitted with a lacrosse stick for additional reach he saw himself as a possible retriever should 715 drop in the enclosure.

Chief Nok-A-Homa's true name is Levi Walker. His Indian blood is Ottawa-Chippewa. He gets paid $8,500 a year by the Braves for what he does—his personal appearances around Georgia on their behalf, his war dance on the pitcher's mound before each game, his whooping exhortations, echoing loonlike among the empty blue seats, and for driving the bullpen pitchers through a gate in the outfield fence to the mound in a 1929 Model A Ford equipped with a modern 283 Chevelle engine with automatic transmission ("It's not a bad car though the front end is a little squirrelly"). A year or so back someone (undoubtedly a member of the bullpen crew) put a smoke bomb under the hood which went off halfway to the pitcher's mound and enveloped the car in such a thick cloud that Chief Nok-A-Homa revolved in it a few times before a gust of wind blew enough away so he could get straightened out.

It was not his first experience at the hands of saboteurs. In 1969 his tepee caught fire during a game against the St. Louis Cardinals. Nok-A-Homa has always suspected Joe Torre, the Cardinals' first baseman. The fire was a brisk one and burned out about a third of the tepee despite Nok-A-Homa's desperate attempts to stamp it out with a horsehide shield and then a broom as a helpful rain of beer, Coke and grape was poured down from the ledge above by fans.

His tepee was quite well appointed before the fire. It had a carpet, a small air conditioner, a portable radio, and a folding chair for the chief to relax in when his limbs were weary from supporting him in a semilotus position in front of the tepee door, or he was tired of war-crying.

He is constantly hollering at the opposing left fielder in the hope of causing a lapse of some sort. He told me that he felt he had finally succeeded with one outfielder, Ken Henderson of the San Francisco Giants. "The physical signs are there," he told me. "You can see by the crick in the neck and the way he kicks little stones that he is very aware of someone behind him."

Chief Nok-A-Homa was full of ideas not only for home run 715 but for the opening-day ceremonies—so many that he began to dim in my mind as a ball-retrieving candidate. He had too much to do. Before the game he was going to do his usual war dance on the pitcher's mound, expanding it by performing some gyrations with a fire hoop, and he was going to conclude the dance with a fire-eating act.

"The last time I tried eating fire was ten years ago," he told me. "I'm going to practice, *definitely.* The big trick, of course, is to blow the solution, which is a combination of kerosene and lighter fluid, *out,* and not swallow it."

"Yes," I said.

For the home run he planned to set off blue, red, and white smoke (though the colored smoke hadn't arrived) from the door of his tepee, and then push a button which would electronically fire a spoke-wheeled two-inch bore cannon brightly painted in white and red which had been placed in the enclosure in left center field.

"The cannon's name is 'A Yankee Carol,' " Nok-A-Homa said. I remarked on the oddness of the name, and he explained that the gun had been donated by an Explorer's Post organization which, spurred by Confederate chauvinism, wanted it called "The Yankee Killer."

"I thought that was too brutal a name—and it didn't sit well with me being an Ottawa-Chippewa out of Michigan. So I named it after a girl who helped put the cannon in the truck—Carol—and we christened it with a bottle of Tuborg beer . . . 'A Yankee Carol.' I felt that 'The' was too individualistic. So it's called 'A.' "

I asked him how he felt he had a chance at catching the ball with all those commitments.

He said that he felt that his chances for the ball were excellent. "I've got my old lacrosse stick. Now, I don't want to hurt none of them, but I'll guarantee I'll be among them. I'm *tall* with that stick."

"Are you frightened that someone might topple down on you from the stands?"

"That's a possibility," Nok-A-Homa said. "A couple of years back we had some drunken fan from Chicago who took a wild leap from the stands trying to get a ball. He broke his back."

There was little doubt there would be mayhem if the ball landed up in the stands. Last year, the Braves' officials told me, a man named A. W. Kirby from Old Hickory, Tennessee, sprinted down an aisle, dove over a chair, and after suffering a broken fingernail and lacerated wrists and ankles in a tremendous scuffle came up with home run 693. He thought the ball was worth $1,700. His son had misinformed him.

The abrasions and thumps suffered in the pileup over 715 would be worth it. The official high was $25,000 (the anonymous Venezuelan fan had been matched by Sammy Davis, Jr., though rumors abounded that even higher offers had come in). The retriever would be photographed giving it back to Aaron, and his or her face would shine out of the country's sports pages, and even if on the periphery, he would know something of the excitement of being touched by the moment.

Eventually the prize would go to the Hall of Fame at Cooperstown, New York (even the big-money bidders had promised this, though no one was positive about the Venezuelan), to join other great talismans of baseball history under their domes of glass—among others Roger Maris's 61st and Babe Ruth's 714th, each with the name of the retriever included.

There are a couple of astonishing things about Ruth's last home run—among others, that it was ever recovered at all. I looked it all up. It was the *third* he hit on that day (May 25, 1935), and it was the first hit completely out of Forbes Field since its construction in 1909, an accomplishment which stood until the 1950s when Ted Beard, a Pirate outfielder, was the first of a select few, including Willie Stargell who did it a couple of times, to join him.

The Pirate pitcher on the mound that day against the Boston Braves (with whom Ruth was finishing his career as a ballplayer) was Guy Bush, who had come in to relieve the starter, Red Lucas, off whom Ruth had hit the first of his trio. Bush now lives on a farm in Mississippi. I managed to find his phone number and called him up to chat about Ruth.

It turned out he had pitched to Ruth twice before— both times in the 1932 Yankees-Cubs World Series (the one in which Ruth hit his fabled "called-shot" home run into the center-field bleachers). In the opener of that series Bush said that he had retired

Ruth (he referred to him as "the Big Bamboo") on his first two times at bat. He got him to hit soft ground balls. But then George Sewall ("a lil' ol' fellah raised down here in the South") hit a drive back through the pitcher's box that busted open the index finger of Bush's right hand and forced his removal from the game.

So it was not until late in the series that he faced Ruth again. This time Bush decided to start off by low-decking him.

"Why did you want to do that?" I asked.

"I had no respect for *any* batter," Bush told me. In the background, over the phone, I could hear the murmur of what sounded like a local television news broadcast. Bush raised his voice: "I wanted no part of any of them, Ruth included. I never spoke to an opposing player for the ten years I played in the major leagues 'cept to shout at 'em from the top step of the dugout. None of them liked me, sir, if you want to know the truth about it."

"So you knocked Ruth down?"

"I throwed to *scare* him. He couldn't get out of the way and I hit him on the arm. I'm sorry of it now. I'd like to take that pitch back."

"He didn't react in any way?"

"Well, he got to second base on an infield out. There was some sort of time-out and he walked halfway to the pitcher's mound. He called to me, 'Hey, *Bush*'—and he said 'Bush' like he was referring to a bush-league player—'if you're going to *hit* anyone, put something on it.' "

A dry chuckle rose from that distant TV set, a man's hollow-sounding laugh at some unheard joke.

"I never answered him," Bush was saying. "Like I told you, sir, I never spoke to anyone on an opposing team—all those years."

"How did one pitch to him?" I asked.

"The book was to keep moving the ball around the plate and you might be lucky. In Pittsburgh, there in Forbes Field that last game in 1935, I threw him a screwball the first time he came up against me, low and outside. He swung and missed it by 18 inches.

Well, sir, he missed it by so much that I thought maybe he had a blind spot and that maybe he couldn't *see* a ball thrown there. Well, that was very exciting. So I threw the same pitch in the same spot and he swung and came very near killing my second baseman.

"The next time I decided to throw a slow curve. Well, sir, I threw the slow curve and he hit this little Chinese home run down the right-field line which was no distance at all, 20 feet back into the stands for his second of the day. He'd hit his first off Lucas. That made me so mad that when he came up again at the back end of the game I called Tommy Padden, my catcher, out to the mound, and I said, 'Tommy, I don't think the Big Bamboo can hit my fast ball.' I *didn't* think so, sir. He had a stance at the plate where he near had his back to the pitcher; he was so far turned around that I could see the number 3 on his uniform; I didn't think the monkey could come around quick enough on my fast ball to get his bat on it. So I told Tommy that I was going to challenge him with the fast ball. In fact, I told Tommy to go back and *tell* the Big Bamboo what I was going to do, that I was going to *damn* him to hit my fast ball. That's how confident I was. Now Tommy Padden has passed away, poor soul, and I can't tell you for sure whether he told the Bamboo what I was going to do. But I can tell you this, sir, that I threw two fast balls and he hit the second one for the longest ball I ever saw. It cleared those whole three decks, and I was too surprised to be mad anymore."

According to the record, the ball Ruth hit sailed over the heads of a group of boys who happened to be standing at the corner of Bouquet and Joncaire and bounced into a construction lot where it was retrieved by a youngster named Henry (Wiggy) Diorio. He took it around to the Schenley Hotel where the Braves were staying, for Ruth's autograph. At that time no one, much less the Babe (he decided to retire a few weeks later) knew that the ball would be the last he would ever hit out of a ball park; he autographed the ball for young Wiggy and said that as far as he was concerned it was just another home run.

As for Roger Maris's 61st home run, that was caught by a young truck driver named Sal Durante. He saw the ball begin its ride, and he hopped up on his seat (number 3 in box 163D in section 33 of Yankee Stadium) and made a one-hand grab. He shouted, "I got it! I got it!" and was immediately engulfed by a tide of fans trying to wrest the ball away. The ball was worth $5,000 to him, put up by a West Coast restaurateur to buy the ball for Maris. It was a pleasant windfall for Durante (who was going to present the ball to Maris anyway) and made his stadium seat, according to the *New York Times* the next day, the most "profitable in baseball history."

Durante got married soon after he caught the ball. The $5,000 proceeds came in very handy. He had to deliver the ball to the Sacramento restaurateur in person to pick up his money. He was so petrified he might lose the ball that he thought of sending it to Sacramento by registered mail.

"If I lose the ball, it's all over for us," he said at the time.

I had found his phone number through the Yankees (who sent him season tickets for a couple of years after the event) and called him up to see how he had fared since. He told me that catching Maris's home run ranked along with his marriage and the births of his children (he has three) as the most exciting moment of his life. It hadn't marked him with much good luck though (he'd tried to make a go of it in Florida, but hadn't, and was out of work when I called him), but the home run was good to think back on, and sometimes things came of it. When the Seattle Exposition opened in 1962, the promoters asked him to come out and try to catch a ball dropped from the Space Needle by Tracy Stallard, who had given up the home run to Maris and was there playing for a minor-league club called the Seattle Rainiers. Durante was to get $1,000 if he caught the ball. Dropping it from the Space Needle proved to be too dangerous; speculation was that Durante might be driven into the ground like a spike. So Tracy Stallard went up in a Ferris wheel about 100 feet or so, and after five practice drops which Durante caught cleanly, the circle of photographers got their gear set and the official toss was signaled.

Durante dropped it!

"I blew it and couldn't believe it," he told me. "The glove they gave me wasn't the best and the ball bounced off the heel. Of course, you must realize," he said, "that I hadn't had much practice . . ."

The Observer

Everything was set and triggered to go off. Behind the center-field stands, out on Capitol Avenue, $2,000 worth of fireworks were set in their mortar pipes just off the sidewalk—collected from four different fireworks manufacturers by a parent outfit in Saginaw, Michigan, which had been lined up by the Braves' management to stay on hand in Atlanta until Aaron produced. Their representative had packed a couple of suitcases for a long stay. He listened to the game on a transistor radio; close at hand was an electric switch which would detonate the entire show. A couple of policemen were with him to stop the traffic as soon as Milo Hamilton, the Braves' announcer, said the ball was gone. The fireworks were set up just a few feet from the highway and it struck me what an odd reaction would be caused in someone driving along Capitol Avenue who didn't happen to be aware of the commotion over Aaron, listening to a Bach cantata on the car radio's FM band, say, when suddenly, right at hand, a whole lawn would light up in a massive thrust of pyrotechnics.

"Doesn't everyone in Atlanta know about Aaron?" said the fireworks representative when I mentioned this fancy to him.

"Just about. I suppose so," I said.

"I'm not so concerned about frightening people driving along the highway," he said. "What worries me is that I'm going to hear the home run wrong . . . that Milo Hamilton is going to shout, 'There it goes!' and then it *won't*, the wind will hold it up or something, or it'll curve foul, and I'll already have thrown the switch. I've come close to doing that before—and once those babies are going up, there's nothing you can do to bring them back."

Inside the ball park—which was filled to capacity an hour before the game to watch the Salute to Aaron—the playing field had been specially doctored. A huge red, white, and blue map of the United States had been painted in short center field—so that, as someone pointed out, a Texas League single could indeed drop on Texas.

When the ceremonies began, designated people out of Aaron's past were driven onto the field by car to stand symbolically on the map at the spot marking important events in the player's life—as Milo Hamilton intoned a commentary over the public-address system. Aaron's parents were presented and took a stand about where Mobile is, his hometown; Ed Scott, who had signed Aaron to the Clowns, was driven out to Indianapolis; John Mullen, the Braves' scout who first recommended him, to Milwaukee; Donald Davidson to Bradenton, Florida, where the Braves had their training camp and Aaron first got into the lineup when the regular left-fielder, Bobby Thomson, broke his ankle. Girls carrying signs with Aaron's milestone hits and home runs began to run onto the map to stand where he had done them—the 200 sign to St. Louis, the 300 to New York, the 400 to Philadelphia; the area around Atlanta began to look like a bus-line queue as the girls with signs including the 500th, 600th, and 700th began to gather there.

The vast field began to seem cluttered. A drill team performed. A band played. A choir appeared, marching out toward second base, the brisk wind snapping their long black gowns back against their bodies as they came, outlining them, so that collectively they looked

like a caucus of heroines materializing off the paper-
back covers of gothic novels.

During all this, out beyond the wire fence in right
field Al Downing toiled away at his warm-up. I could
see the red 44 on the back of his grey uniform flash as
he spun in his delivery. The same number as Aaron's.
He was working hard out there. How could all this
hoopla *not* affect him? After all, the ceremony was
simply a buildup to the dramatic confrontation in which
he was an integral part, indeed the figure who would
appear at a climactic moment to assist in the grand
finale. The music and the ceremonial going-to-and-fro
(and now the report shells bursting noisily above the
center-field fence) were all curtain-raiser frills to prepare the crowd for this sacrificial moment—what the
fighting bull hears on the other side of the *toril* as the
excitement and panoply grow in anticipation of his appearance. Surely this sort of idea must have tugged at
his mind—that he was just as much a functionary in
this inevitable scheme of things as a bandsman peering
at his sheet music and preparing to bang a drum with a
mallet at the appointed moment. It was just a question
of when Downing's *time* was due—perhaps twenty
minutes from now and he would watch Aaron rear up
from his kneeling position in the on-deck circle and
walk slowly toward the plate, carrying his batting helmet in his hand. He would turn to polish up the ball—
a sigh would escape him, and his catcher, going out to
commiserate, would hear him say, "Well, it's almost
over."

Nonsense, of course. But it was the sort of thing that
occurred to me standing there as the darkness came
down and the natural light of the evening gave way to
the fluorescentlike bath that seemed to cleanse the stadium in the night games into sharp definition, the white
bases and the chalk lines almost blinding, like beach
sand at noon, every blade of grass in the infield glistening, every face, those vast banks of them, parchment
clean—indeed an artificial glow in which any sort of
theatrics seemed possible.

Down on the field next to the Braves' dugout I stood

next to Tony Kubek, the ex-Yankee who is now a broadcaster for NBC. We looked out at Downing. Kubek remembered that he was found asleep on a training table just before he was to pitch the opening game in the 1963 World Series.

"He had a strange sort of sleeping-sickness disease," Kubek said. "It was called narcolepsy, which is vaguely related to sleeping sickness. Later they diagnosed it at the Mayo Clinic. It's rather common and you can get medication for it."

The reverberations from the aerial bombs echoed in the stadium.

"I'll guarantee you he's not sleepy now," Kubek said.

Aaron stayed in the dugout during the first part of the ceremony. It must have been impossible to hear anything in there. He sat in the back of the dugout joking with his teammates. It almost looked as though he had to be coaxed to run out onto the field for his part in the proceedings. Milo Hamilton had to come to the top of the dugout steps to fetch him. Aaron gestured to the player he'd been talking with, almost as if to suggest he was going to be right back—"just a moment while I get this done and over with"—and he and Hamilton began to trot through an alley of crossed bats held up by two rows of girls wearing white T-shirts and shorts. I could hear his words over the loudspeaker system; shredded by the wind and strangely subdued after the high-hype quality of the commentary preceding. He said, "I just hope I can get this thing over with tonight—as soon as possible."

"Think of that," someone next to me was saying, "he thinks of it all as a 'thing.' "

When the field was finally cleared, game time imminent, Chief Nok-A-Homa made his appearance. He came running out to the pitcher's mound carrying a flaming hoop; his cheeks were puffed out by his home brew, which he had enough of tucked away to produce three grand puffs of flame. The crowd roared. He put his head and shoulders through the hoop, and drew it down over his body, stepping out of it like a girl getting out of a skirt. Following his war dance on the pitcher's mound he raced for his tepee in the left-field corner, carrying his hoop aloft like an Olympic torch. After him, far in his wake after having climbed the steps of the Braves' dugout, came his five-year-old son, Hit-A-Single, in moccasins and regalia, dwarfed in that enormous expanse, so that his chugging advance seemed just barely to carry him along—a remote, small figure, like someone spotted in a vast meadow from a high-flying helicopter. When he finally disappeared the field was empty, waiting, and the thousands in the stands staring down at it began to roar in anticipation . . .

The Observer

Aaron came up in the second inning. I sat on the front step of the aisle in the left-field stands. I wondered where to look—some vector of my attention which might tell me more about the moment, if it came, than if I observed Aaron directly. That was what Ernest Hemingway said about watching baseball games—that something other than the action itself would provide the best key to a description of value. The rain was still falling slightly.

I concentrated on Aaron. I didn't have the discipline to look elsewhere. Downing was very careful with him. He threw two balls, one of them into the dirt, then got a called strike. Now another ball, and the count was 3–1. The crowd bellowed its dismay. I found my notepaper shaking in my hand. He had a true chance now —the count completely in his favor if Downing had any thought of keeping him off the base paths with a walk. He had not taken the bat off his shoulders. Downing fussed a bit, and as if the possibility was too much to bear, he turned and fired a ball outside and Aaron had walked.

The Hitter

Aaron came up for the second time in the fourth inning. He had yet to swing the bat off his shoulder at a ball. Downing's first pitch was a change-up that puffed in the dirt in front of the plate. The umpire, Satch Davidson, looked at it suspiciously through the bars of his mask and tossed it out. He signaled to Frank Pulli, the first-base umpire, to throw in another of the specially marked balls, this one identified with a 12, stamped twice in invisible ink, and two 2's. Downing polished it up a bit, turned, and as the clock on the scoreboard showed 9:07 he wheeled and delivered a fast ball, aiming low and expecting it to tail away on the outside corner.

The ball rose off Aaron's bat in the patented trajectory of his long hits, ripping out over the infield, the shortstop instinctively bending his knees as if he could leap for it, and it headed for deep left center field.

From behind the plate Satch Davidson leaned over the catcher Joe Ferguson's shoulder, and as the two stood up to watch the flight of the ball going out, the umpire said, "Fergie, that might be it." The catcher said, "I think so too."

Out in left center field Jimmy Wynn, who often plays with a toothpick working in his mouth, and Bill Buckner converged on the ball. The pair of them had a vague hope that if the ball was going over, somehow Buckner was going to scale the fence and get to the ball before anyone else; he would toss it back over the fence, and the two of them were going to split the reward. Afterward, his toothpick whisking busily in his mouth, Wynn admitted that the two of them would doubtless have given the ball to Aaron: "We wanted him to get it over with, so he could be a human being again."

At the time, though, Buckner made a leap up the

fence, scaling up it with his spikes in the wire mesh until, spread-eagled for an instant like a gigantic moth against a screen door, he saw that he had no chance, and he dropped back down.

Aaron never saw the ball clear the fence. As he had done those countless times, he looked toward first base as he ran, dropping his bat neatly just off the base path, and when he saw the exultation of the first-base coach, Jim Busby, he knew for sure that the long chase was over.

The Fan

Most of the home runs hit to left field do not reach the stands. They land in the bullpen enclosure. Last season, as Aaron crept toward the record, and each home-run ball became more valuable, the bullpen crew would stand up and fan out along the fence. As I watched from above, the most intense of them struck me as Maximino Leon. At each pitch from the faraway mound he went up on his toes like an infielder.

He was the loner on the pitching staff. He could not speak more than a word or so of English. Indeed on one occasion he went to an Atlanta dentist to have a tooth removed and had nineteen extracted before he could muster up enough English to complain. But he knew about the home runs and their value, and he was always up, when Aaron was at the plate, inching down toward the left-center area, and it always seemed to me that it would be nip-and-tuck between him and Chief Nok-A-Homa.

Noting Leon's obvious eagerness, and the more subdued though nonetheless absorbed interest of the other players in the bullpen, who rose and crept along the fence with feigned nonchalance when Aaron came to bat, it was decided by the Braves' management that the whole procedure ought to be policed—in case in the general scuffle over an Aaron home run landing in the enclosure someone might get hurt, even by a fan toppling on him from the ledge above.

So Ken Silvestri, the bullpen coach, was given the job. He considers himself something of an expert on special balls of this sort—remembering the opening-day ceremonies when the "first ball" was tossed into a group rather than to a catcher, as it is now, and if the ball was tossed by a particular luminary, such as President Roosevelt, a melee invariably occurred which often involved violent shoving and spiked ankles. It was a free-for-all, sort of like throwing a bone into a heavily populated kennel.

He decided to spot his bullpen crew (consisting besides himself of two catchers, five relief pitchers—not including Leon, who had been optioned to Richmond in the Braves' farm system—and Gary Gentry, scheduled to pitch the next day) at intervals along the fence toward center field. Having sent everyone to his position, Silvestri stationed himself under the roof of the shed where the bullpen staff sit for protection from the elements. He was hoping Aaron in his eagerness was going to pull it more down the foul lines than he usually does. In the fourth inning, with Aaron up for the second time, he looked around for the big flexible mitt catchers use to handle knuckle balls and discovered that Gary Gentry, a *pitcher* what's more, had swiped it, leaving Silvestri with the regular catcher's glove, which is not the best piece of equipment to catch a long drive. He was just about to call across and cuss out Gentry when Downing began his wind-up and threw . . .

The Announcer

At the sound of the ball hitting the bat, quite distinct before being violently submerged by the massive roar from the fans, the chief voice of the

Atlanta Braves rose in the broadcast booth against the tumult to describe the event over the air to the outside world. The voice belonged to Atlanta's local broadcaster, Milo Hamilton, formerly an announcer for the White Sox and the Cubs. It was a tremendous moment for him. True, the NBC crew was on hand for the Monday night baseball broadcast (Curt Gowdy, Tony Kubek, and Joe Garagiola) and so was Vince Scully, the Dodger announcer for the past 25 years, broadcasting the game back to Los Angeles. Through their combined media over 35 million people would see or hear the instant, but none had a more personal involvement than Milo Hamilton; being with the Braves he was the only broadcaster in the country who had known for months that at some point he would be describing Aaron's historic home run—which made his situation enviable for a sports broadcaster. While he had to verbalize instantly into a microphone what he saw, in the case of Aaron's great home run, since it was inevitable, Hamilton had a chance to prepare a sentence so perfect that if it worked, if enough people heard it and commented on it, it had a fine chance to slip into Bartlett's Quotations alongside "One small step . . ." etc.

I was intrigued by the possibility. We talked about it quite a lot. Hamilton told me that he wasn't going to work at anything very ornate, but that he certainly had something planned. He wouldn't tell me what it was. I asked him if he would write the sentence down and slip it into an envelope which I wouldn't open until after the home run had been hit. No, he said, he'd as soon keep it to himself.

I looked into Bartlett's Quotations myself to see if I could find anything that might inspire Hamilton in his search. As phrases to drop into the general hubbub of exaltation I rather liked Cicero's "What a time! What a civilization!" and Horace's "This day I've lived!" My favorite was an extension of William Wordsworth: "There's not a man who lives who hath not known his godlike hours—and here is Aaron's!" I resisted handing them on to Hamilton.

Milo Hamilton has a small cherubic face out of which one might expect a choirboy's voice; instead, he rumbles in the orotund throatal tones of the true broadcaster, which a friend of mine in the television industry refers to as a "four-ball" voice. It was hard not to be solemn, equipped with such a voice. His earliest idol as he grew up in Iowa was Bob Elson, who broadcast the Chicago White Sox games for almost forty years—a span which had seen (Hamilton felt) a drift from straight reporting to showmanship. "I like to think of myself as a meld of the professionalism of Bob Elson and the enthusiasm of Harry Caray, the sportscaster for the White Sox." He had told me that he had especially hoped that 715 would be hit in Atlanta. "We have a television blackout for home games, so I'll be on radio. On radio a sportscaster really has to paint a picture, and it's always been one of my great rewards that I get a lot of praise from blind people."

I told him I was reminded of the one time I had been allowed to broadcast a bit of a Yankee game on radio, much of which was taken up with "painting a picture" of a foul ball bouncing into the opposing team's dugout. I happened to be a guest in the broadcasting booth and Phil Rizzuto, almost on impulse, pushed the radio microphone in front of me to let me try to describe a half inning.

I had a preconception of what it was going to be like; it is common enough, I suppose, to pretend to broadcast a sporting event—at least *I* find myself doing it at tennis matches and baseball games when the action is slow . . . my lips moving slightly, the words intoned just softly enough not to catch the attention of the spectators in the vicinity: *the pitch . . . Jones lifts a long fly toward . . .*

Faced with an actual situation I eagerly began with a long and extremely detailed description of the first thing that happened—a foul ball: I did a thorough description of its passage past the on-deck circle: "It's rolling along there toward the top step of the dugout and it doesn't . . . quite . . . get there. No sir, it stops two or three feet from the dugout, and there it is, and someone has reached out and *picked it up*, can't see who it is, and it's gone. That's right. It's gone into the dugout somewhere . . ." etc.

Phil Rizzuto listened to this patiently.

"Who's up?" I whispered to him.

"The same man," he said. "Nettles."

Nettles then lifted a fly and as it rose above the rim of the stadium I lost it in a white haze. I admitted as much into the microphone.

"I've lost it. Where did it go?"

Rizzuto leaned over the microphone to help me out. "Watch the fielders," he said.

They were converging in right center field. "Jackson is under it in right," he said. "And he has it."

Hamilton listened solemnly. "I'm relieved I don't have you as a partner in the booth," he said. "After those fouls you wouldn't have enough emotion left for the important moments."

The other man on the broadcast team was Ernie Johnson—a former pitcher for the Braves during the "good" years in the mid-fifties, a New Englander with a somewhat more folksy, down-to-earth quality than Hamilton. By chance he was on the radio when Aaron hit home runs 500, 600, and 700—much to Hamilton's dismay. The regular procedure on radio had been for Hamilton to hand over the microphone for the third and seventh innings, and it was during these innings that Aaron hit those monumental home runs. It was a cause of considerable merriment among the Braves' management, and indeed with listeners, to note Hamilton's care not to be caught short again. Since the 700th home run, if Aaron happened to come to bat in the third or seventh inning, Ernie Johnson's voice would suddenly give way to Milo Hamilton's familiar oratory. One could imagine a struggle up in the booth between the two of them over the microphone, hauling it back and forth between them, but Johnson was not only the junior partner but resigned, and rather phlegmatic about the situation.

Hamilton, on the other hand, feels that his entire career has been building toward the instant of Aaron's 715th. He has already had some climactic games to describe. They include a pair of no-hitters, one by Tooth-pick Sam Jones in May 1955, who walked the first three Pirate batters he faced in the ninth inning and had to talk manager Stan Hack, who stood on the pitcher's mound reaching for the ball, out of removing him; he stayed in to strike out the side. The other no-hitter was pitched by the Braves' knuckleballer, Phil Niekro; Hamilton still remembers his exact wording over the air as the last man up grounded a ball into the infield: "If he gets the man at first, it's a no-hitter *(pause)*. And it *is!*"

I asked him if that had been prearranged—if he had decided on that conceit if it happened he should de-scribe a no-hitter.

He said not at all—that spontaneity was always the key to sportscasting. "It's very much my cup of tea. It has to be everybody's."

A consideration of important moments in sports re-porting would bear him out. The most common char-acteristic, since the description is made under pressure and against the crowd noise, is that key sentences are often repeated, such as the flurry of repetitions when Russ Hodges, ordinarily a somewhat low-keyed sports-caster, gave his on-the-spot report of Bobby Thomson's "miracle of Coogan's Bluff" home run in the Dodger-Giant play-off game in 1951: "The Giants win the pennant! The Giants win the pennant! The Giants win the pennant! The Giants win the pennant! I don't be-lieve it! I don't believe it! I DO NOT BELIEVE IT!"

Describing the extraordinary home run of Ted Wil-liams in his last time at bat in the majors (as neat a punctuation to his career as an exclamation point) Curt Gowdy had a brace of repeated sentences: "It's got a chance! It's got a chance! And it's gone . . ." all of this, in fact, in somewhat restrained fashion since in an earlier inning Williams had hit a long fly ball which Gowdy described as if it were going into the seats; he did not want to be fooled again.

Phil Rizzuto, the Yankee sportscaster, had a quasi-opportunity much like Hamilton's to prepare for Roger Maris's 61st home run, which was a strong possibility though hit on the last day of the season. Obviously, he did not do so, since his radio commentary, utilizing his favorite epithet, was absolutely predictable. "Holy cow!" he cried. "That's gonna be it."

Red Barber remembers that when he was broadcasting the famous Cookie Lavagetto double that destroyed Yankee Bill Bevens's no-hitter in the 1947 World Series, he described the high drive and how it hit the fence, and here came the tying run and now the winning run, and here was Lavagetto being mobbed by his own teammates, and near beaten-up, and then Barber gave a sigh, worn out by all the drama, and he said memorably, "Well, I'll be a suck-egg mule."

Television broadcasting, obviously, gives the announcer a better chance to drop in a *bon mot,* since the picture on the set, if the technicians are on their toes, portrays so much. When Barber was the television commentator on the day that Roger Maris broke Ruth's 60-home-runs-in-a-year record, he started out, "It's a high fly ball . . ." and he paused, noting on the TV monitor that the flight of the ball was clearly shown, and then remembering that a Los Angeles restaurateur had offered a large sum of money for the ball, he announced when it dropped into the stands: "It's 61 and $5,000!"

I spoke to a number of sportscasters about describing the Aaron home run. Joe Garagiola was in Atlanta. He said what he felt many announcers would do: let the crowd take over. He told me about broadcasting Mickey Mantle's 500th home run, over which there had been considerable buildup and hoopla. When he heard the "awful" sound of the ball hitting the bat (as a former catcher Garagiola was acutely responsive to that doom-ridden sound—"awful" was how he described it) he cried "It's gone!" and backed off the microphone and let the huge crowd roar dramatize the moment. Afterward people came up to tell him to his astonishment, "Boy, what a great job you did on that home run. Wow!"

I asked him about Milo Hamilton's thought of preparing a deathless phrase.

"I don't see how you can prepare anything . . . 'a giant step for the horsehide' . . . No, I don't think so."

Howard Cosell said it was not his method either. When I telephoned him, I started by asking him if he ever constructed a dramatic scene in his mind, a superlative round in a heavyweight championship, say, and practiced by pretending to be on hand doing the play-by-play announcing. He said that no, he didn't. Frankly he never thought of himself as a play-by-play announcer. He spoke with some testiness, as if I had irked him by suggesting that he had anything to do with play-by-play. He was what he referred to as a "reporter-commentator."

"The play-by-play announcer is a parrot," he went on. "He performs only slightly more of a function than the public-address announcer. 'A bouncing ball to short . . . the throw across to first . . .' what else is there to say. In television the play-by-play announcer is becoming obsolete."

"If you were broadcasting on radio, how would you describe the Aaron home run?" I asked.

"The noise and excitement of the crowd will carry that instant," Cosell replied, affirming what Garagiola had said. "What I would probably do—of course it depends on the *feel* of the moment—is to comment on the growth of Aaron the man as well as Aaron the baseball player. I'd splice in my memories—Aaron's relationship with his managers—Bobby Bragan and Eddie Mathews, and how riding back from Ebbets Field with Jackie Robinson one day, I heard him say that number 44 would one day be a greater player than he or Willie Mays but that he had no feeling for him as a *man*. Finally, before he died, he *did*, you know—Robinson could see that Aaron was coming out of the shell, the shyness which was really the reason he was so obscure despite his brilliance . . . and beginning to *try*, at least, to deal with the issues that Robinson felt every black was compelled to. The growth of Aaron as a person—that's the sort of thing I would have dealt with."

The other broadcaster I talked to in the pressroom on the evening of the game was Vince Scully. He is the Los Angeles Dodgers' "voice" and has been so for the last 25 years . . . in fact so long that he said as we sat down over coffee that he felt like a man who's observed everything, seen Halley's comet—at least as far as baseball was concerned, and was running out of records to watch set.

"I've seen Maury Wills beat Ty Cobb's base-stealing record; Don Drysdale's 56 consecutive scoreless innings streak. Every time I saw Hoyt Wilhelm pitch he was extending Cy Young's old record of number of pitching appearances. Larsen's perfect game . . ."

"What did you say when he threw the final pitch?" I asked.

"Larsen? Yes. To Dale Mitchell. A called strike. I cried out: 'Perfect game!!' "

"Was that the most dramatic?"

Scully shook his head. "The only time I ever got carried away and became rather ultraformal was in 1955 when the Dodgers finally won the World Series." Scully leaned back. " 'Peewee Reese straightens up to throw . . . ladies and gentlemen, the Brooklyn Dodgers are the champions of the world!' "

A number of the press craned around to look at us. His voice had boomed out into the room.

"But that wasn't prepared," he told me, leaning in across the table. "That was pure emotion."

Curt Gowdy, the head of the NBC broadcast crew, had a different reason for not cluttering up the mind with key phrases.

"What every sportscaster is truly scared of is anticipating something that doesn't happen," he said. "Why, suppose the Aaron homer starts going out and the guy unleashes the great sentence he's been working on for two months and the ball ends up in an outfielder's glove. It happens more than you think. I won't ever be *allowed* to forget a tremendous hit that was slugged by Hoot Evers with the bases loaded in Shibe Park in Philadelphia in 1952 . . . just soaring for the upper deck, and I could see Gus Zernial, the outfielder, watching it go with his hands on his hips practically, and that's the way you tell—watch the fielder—and I shouted, 'There it goes! A grand slammer!'

"Something happened to it up there—a gust of wind, perhaps, that knocked it down like a dying bird, and

Gus Zernial, who told me later that he was almost as surprised as I was, put his glove up and hauled it in. Well, I had to retract. I told them, 'Fans, I really blew it,' and Tom Yawkey, who owned the Red Sox, kidded me for five years about that.

"Well, that's the sort of thing that absorbs the mind of the sportscaster. He hasn't got the capacity to carry prepared phrases around in his mind if he's got that sort of responsibility to worry about."

All the broadcasters seem to have had disasters of this sort. Mel Allen once told me about describing a tremendous drive Mickey Mantle hit out over the bleachers which he felt had been slugged hard enough to carry out of Yankee Stadium—for the first time ever—and losing sight of it as it started to drop from its enormous height he watched to see if the people in the bleachers scrambled for it. Nobody moved. Heads were looking back. That was enough for Allen. He cried: "It's out of the ball park—first time in history."

It turned out that a man sitting with his back to the wall had caught the ball as he sat there—catching it cleanly (and with considerable aplomb, one would assume, without moving a jot on his bleacher seat) so that the quick rush of scramblers which would indicate to Allen that the ball was still in the park never occurred.

Sometimes the reverse happens. Charley Jones, who is the chief Cincinnati Reds' announcer, once got caught on what he described as a routine fly ball ("there's a fly ball to right field") which suddenly landed deep in the pavilion and Jones was forced to shift gears abruptly in his commentary.

I told Milo Hamilton about these conversations—that all his peers felt that prearranging anything was *suspect,* to say the least. Hamilton said that he was certainly tempted to agree with them, and *would* ordinarily, but that on his speaking tour that past winter he realized that so much curiosity was being generated by what he was going to say at the climactic moment that he felt bound to work something up.

In the evenings he would sit around and let his imagination take over; as he watched the Aaron home run arch into the seats, his lips murmured; the sentences formed; the facts crowded his mind, especially the similarities between Aaron and Babe Ruth . . . that both were born just a day apart in February, both hitting the 714th home run at the same age (40) and both as members of the Braves' organization. He had toyed with the idea of announcing much of this material as Aaron circled the bases after hitting 715, using each base as marker along the way (". . . he steps on *second* . . . and the Babe's great record, nearly twoscore years old . . . and he steps on *third* . . . a great day for Aquarians! Both Henry and the Babe . . .").

"And the big sentence?" I asked. "Just as he whacks it."

"I'm not going to tell you. You'll have to wait and see."

The Observer

I watched 715 go over the fence while sitting back in the left-field corner. I had taken a quick look to either side—at the rows of faces in perfect profile, poised in expectation, jaws slightly dropped, a gallery leaning slightly forward off their seats in the ashen light of the arcs. Then, almost as one, everybody stood up.

I'd never heard a sound like that. My notes show that a seismograph scribble was the best I could do to describe that sustained pitch—absolutely constant, so that after a while it seemed caught inside the head, like a violent hum in the ears.

While this uproar was going on, all around I saw arms raised in every form of salute . . . clenched fists, V's for victory, arms pumped up and down. Below in left field, I could see Jimmy Wynn, the Dodgers' left fielder. He had his glove off and he was clapping. In center field Bill Buckner was shaking his fist in triumph.

In the distance Downing headed for the dugout. He sat down and looked out on the festivities as detached as an old man watching children play from his park bench. No one seemed to cluster around, or even look at him. Motionless, the bills of the Dodgers' baseball caps pointed out to the field.

After the ceremonies at home plate, Downing came back out. His control problems, which had gotten him into the mess, had not been helped by the layover, and he walked the first two batters. Walter Alston relieved him. It seemed proper somehow—that the small left-hander, having supplied the dramatic moment (almost as if he and Aaron had breakfasted together to master-mind this engineering feat), should be allowed to depart to the wings.

The Pitcher

Downing went to the empty Dodger locker room and dressed. A taxi was ordered for him and he stood out in the stadium tunnel waiting for it. The game was still on and Milo Hamilton's voice murmured from the amplifying system in the visiting-team locker room. I was coming along the tunnel and I happened to spot him. He was in a coal black jump-suit outfit, with a black felt belt looped around his waist, and he was wearing black shoes polished to a glisten. I went up and said I was sorry that it had happened to him. He has a very cheery voice which seems to bely the gravity of any situation one might connect him with . . .

"Well, that's that," he said. "I didn't have the rhythm and the fast ball wasn't doing what it was supposed to, which is to drop slightly. I threw a change-up, low, and then I threw a fast ball right down the middle—the best possible pitch if it had done what it was supposed to. There was a man on base. Since my fast ball sinks—usually!—there was every reason to believe he would bang it along the ground for a double-play possibility. That's what Satchel Paige always said: 'With men on base, throw the ball low and let the infielders do the work for you.' What did I think when he hit it? 'Damn, there goes our lead!' So I went and sat in the dugout. Nobody said anything about the home run. Why should they? We're all grown men. We don't have to console each other. One or two people came by and said, 'We'll get the runs back for you.' "

It was awkward talking to him—one wanted to commiserate and assure him that the whole thing was nonsense, and yet one had the notebook that flipped back on itself, and the pencil poised.

"What about the catcher?" I asked merrily. "I mean he was the guy who called for the pitch."

Downing laughed. "I'm the guy who's going to have to live with the ramifications. It was a fine call—a good idea."

I asked him if all the pregame commotion had bothered him—the fireworks banging away. He grinned. "So those were fireworks. I was wondering. I couldn't see from the bullpen."

A photographer appeared with a small souvenir placard handed out by the Braves testifying that the bearer had been on hand to see the record home run hit. It had a picture of Aaron and the number 715. The photographer wanted Downing to pose with it, hold it up, and smile.

Downing shook his head quickly. "I don't think that would prove anything." He looked up and down the tunnel for his taxi.

"Is it going to bother you much?" I asked.

"I've been around too many great athletes, and observed them, to kick the water cooler and throw things," he said. "If Whitey Ford had a bad day, he never made excuses or made life embarrassing for others. A lot of players think that if they throw a bat, they're showing that they're competitive. But that's not what I think. A pitcher has to maintain composure. I'm more concerned about my next start," he went on. "This thing is over. It's history. It won't bother me. There's only one home run hit off me that's ever stayed in my mind.

That was the grand-slam home run that Ken Boyer hit off me in the sixth inning of the 1964 World Series that beat the Yankees 4–3 and turned the whole series around. I threw him a change-up, and there was a lot of second-guessing that I had thrown him the wrong pitch, that I should have challenged him. I thought about that for a long time. I was 23 at the time. It was a technical consideration. This one? It's more emotional. Well, pitchers don't ever like to give up home runs. But," he said in the cheery voice, "I'm not giving myself up to trauma. People will be calling to see if I've jumped out the window yet. I'm not going to wake up in the middle of the night and begin banging on the walls, and looking over the sill down into the street. The next time I pitch against him I'll get him out."

A distant roar went up from the crowd. The Braves were having a good inning.

"Your team has made six errors."

"That so? They must be pressing," Downing said. "Everybody's edgy tonight." He craned his head, looking for his taxi.

The Retriever

The last man in line up along the fence toward center field had been the lefthander Tommy House, one of the staff's "short" relievers. He is called "Puma" by his teammates for the way he bounces around during the pepper games and thumps down cat-like on the ball.

The ball came right for him. When he caught it, he raised both his arms in triumph, the white of the ball glistening in his left hand, an enormous bright grin flashed on his face, and he ran for the infield where Aaron was circling the bases.

I tried to see him after the game. His cubicle was banked solid with reporters trying to get a word with

him. Across the way was Chief Nok-A-Homa. I told
the chief that he had been my odds-on candidate for
retrieving the 715 ball.

He laughed and said that he realized he wouldn't
have a chance. Since the bullpen corps was lined up
from his tepee to the "fan-o-gram" board he would have
been obliged to run past the whole bunch, his lacrosse
stick outstretched, and he decided that was unseemly,
and probably dangerous. He had resigned himself to
missing out on the Aaron ball—that is unless it was
lined through the door of his tepee. When Aaron came
to bat, he stood out in front and pumped his lacrosse
stick up and down and whooped a few times, unheard
in the din.

He told me that he was convinced Aaron was going
to hit it that day . . . his Ottawa-Chippewa instincts. As
the ball arched over the fence just down the line from
him, he stood for a moment, tears bursting in his eyes
as his young son, Hit-A-Single, watched him curiously.
Then he rushed inside the tepee to get his smoke bombs
going and to fire off "A Yankee Carol."

His smoke bomb functioned properly. The tepee immediately filled with smoke, which drifted out thickly
through the ventilating hole in the top. I told him I'd
seen it from where I was standing back in the left-field
corner of the stands. Aesthetically, it looked more as if
the tepee had been once again set afire—perhaps by
one of those conniving St. Louis Cardinals. I could see
Nok-A-Homa come out, coughing, as he apparently
reached for the switch that was supposed to set off
"A Yankee Carol" electrically. The cannon waited not
more than six or seven feet from where the ball had
been caught. He hit the switch. A long lazy plume of
smoke puffed out of the muzzle.

"I didn't hear 'A Yankee Carol,' " I said. "I thought
it was going to blow the fence over."

"If there was a noise it was a little *pop*," Nok-A-
Homa said. "The damn thing was a dud. I stared at it
and threw the switch a couple of times to see if I
couldn't get something more out of that damn cannon,
but she just *sat* there. It upset me so much I completely

forgot to do the victory dance that I had especially prepared for the home run."

Across the locker room a large clutch of newsmen had begun to drift away from Tommy House's cubicle. I went over to talk to him. He was sitting on his stool, a slight figure, his face still cheerful with excitement. He took off his baseball shoes and placed them with studied neatness by the side of his cubicle. Behind him I noticed that his locker was fastidiously kept—each hanger evenly spaced, each article on the shelf placed just so. I remarked on it, and he said Yes, it bothered the locker-room boys, who were mother hens and liked to pick up after the ballplayers.

"Quite a day for you," I said. "Did you ever think you might drop the ball out there—I mean muff it?"

"The whole thing blew my mind. The ball came right at me, just rising off the bat on a line. If I'd frozen still like a dummy the ball would have hit me right in the middle of the forehead. Drop the ball?" He shook his head and laughed. "It never occurred to me. It wouldn't to anyone who's been catching fly balls since he was a kid. The only vague problem was someone directly above me who had a fishnet on a pole; he couldn't get it operating in time."

I wondered if he was the fan who'd kept his stepsister tossing up balls for him all that winter for practice.

"Did you ever think of keeping the ball for yourself?" I asked.

"All of us had agreed to turn it in," he said. "I remember going up to Henry and saying that I would give the ball to him if I caught it. He said, 'I appreciate it.' Since then I've been getting a lot of kidding, particularly from the other people out in the bullpen, because I'm studying to get my master's degree in marketing and I don't suppose my professors would give me high marks for opportunism, what with so much being offered for the ball. But I'm not at all sorry. What made it worthwhile was what I saw when I ran in with the ball, holding it in my gloved hand, running really fast—in fact my teammates joked afterward that it was the fastest I'd run in a couple of years—

really just wanting to get rid of it, to put it in Henry's hand. In that great crowd around home plate I found him looking over his mother's shoulder, hugging her to him, and suddenly I saw what many people have never been able to see in him—deep emotion. *I'd* never seen that before in my two years with the club. He has such cool. He never gets excited. He's so *stable.* And I looked and he had tears hanging on his lids. I could hardly believe it. 'Hammer, here it is,' I said. I put the ball in his hand. He said, 'Thanks, kid,' and touched me on the shoulder. I kept staring at him. And it was then that it was brought home to me what his home run meant, not only to him, but to all of us . . .' "

The Fan

The Bill Currys were sitting five or six rows back, just off the corner of the foul screen—terrific seats. Bill Curry plays center for the Houston Oilers. He is the president of the Football Players Association, but he is a great baseball fan. His wife is slim and lively; she is not sure she understands baseball and she is thankful she is married to someone involved in football, which she says she *does* understand. Nonetheless, she had joined her husband and some friends for the opener, and their party had arrived early, during batting practice, to get full benefit of being in on what they all hoped would be an historic evening.

In the third inning, Caroline looked at her scorecard and worked it out in her head that there were seven Braves' batters to appear before Aaron came up for his second at bat—plenty of time for a visit to the rest room and to stop at a refreshment stand. She asked if she could get anyone in the party anything. The man in back of her, who works in an Atlanta real-estate firm, leaned over and said Yes, that was nice of her, he'd very much like a bag of peanuts and a Coke, if it wasn't too much trouble.

About ten people were in line at the refreshment stand. "Everybody seemed a little edgy," she remembered afterward. "The line moved quite quickly, but none of us were prepared for that awful roar that went up. The man in front of me yelled and threw his money down and ran. Some people looked startled; others simply stayed in line; they looked as though they had shut everything out of their minds: they had their hot dogs to get. I ran for the entrance gate. It was clogged with people. I couldn't see. It was too late. It had happened and at the great moment I was leaning forward and about to ask a man for a bag of peanuts. I was terribly mortified. I burst into tears. The man next to me was holding a hot dog. Some mustard had come off on his hand. 'Lady,' he said to me mournfully, 'this is the story of my life.' "

Her husband, Bill, was not especially surprised. "Caroline has an uncanny knack for this sort of thing," he told me later. "If something extraordinary happens—at the ball park, or at the beach, or even at home when something great is said at a party, or has just appeared on the television set, everybody says, 'Gosh that was great!' and then they look around and everybody says, 'Hey, where's Caroline?' "

The Hitter

When the home run lined out over the fence, Donald Davidson—presumably one of many—burst into tears, though no one in the Braves' management, considering him as tough as nails, would believe it, or managed to bear witness to it. He is the club's traveling secretary and a power in its administration. He is a dwarf in stature, having been stunted in his early growth by a form of sleeping sickness. On the day of the game he was wearing a plaid sport coat with a little 715 clip-on button in the lapel. Usually he watches the game from box A in the mezzanine tier, a private box, which is glassed in against the outside, with a thick carpet, and a bar in back, and deep-seated swivel chairs reserved for the Braves' officialdom and their friends, invariably two or three patrician-looking gentlemen in elegantly cut sport coats and gray flannels. They nurse two or three bourbons during a game, and at a good play they rear back to slap their knees and say such things as "Did you see that boy hit that ball? Why I declare he near tore t'other boy's head off!"

Davidson stands off to one side of the box next to a small console desk which is the right size for him to lean on, and on which he keeps his scorecard, and scratch pads on which to scribble himself notes, and there is a phone at hand which connects him with any-place in the stadium. He is very much on top of every-thing; if the count is wrong on the scoreboard, the person responsible will be buzzed and told in broad Bostonian accents to get it right.

He was in the press box when the home run was hit, and almost immediately he received a message from box A that the White House had called; the President wished to congratulate Aaron.

I happened to be standing in the Braves' locker room when Davidson came hustling in. The clubhouse at-tendants were setting big cases of Moët Chandon cham-pagne on tables in the center of the room. Davidson took me aside and said that he had put the White House on hold while he relayed word to Mathews in the dugout. The manager was going to let Henry hurry up to the clubhouse and return the call the next time the Braves came to bat. We waited in Mathews's office, and as Milo Hamilton gave us word of the last Dodger outs in the inning—both locker rooms are wired in to the radio broadcast—Davidson reached for the phone and began to call the White House.

He was proud of what he was doing, and his manner was officious and quite grand—but as so often happens

in such cases he was betrayed . . . in this case by a
telephone operator who was probably the only person
in town unaware of what was going on in the stadium,
and for whom apparently (as best I could decipher
from what Davidson was saying) even baseball itself
was a foreign pursuit.

He began by asking for an operator in Washington;
then reading from a napkin on which he had scribbled
the figure he gave the White House number.

"That's the number of the White House," he said
importantly. He leaned back in his seat. "Yes. In Washington. I'm serious, honey. We're returning a call from
the President of the United States. What? What's the
number here?" He leaned forward and looked at the
dial face of Mathews's telephone. It was blank. "There
doesn't seem to be a number on here, honey. Can't you
connect me with that operator. We're not calling *collect*
or anything. Honey, *we're* the ones who got the call
from the President. We didn't call him. We are returning *his* call. That's right. The President of the United
States. Mr. Aaron is returning President Nixon's call.
He hit a . . . What? No, I'm not Mr. Aaron. He's down
in the dugout, but he's going to be up here any minute.
The dugout? That's where . . . Look honey," he said.
Apparently she had gone off the line. He looked at me
despairingly. When she came back on, he shouted in a
burst of momentary confusion: "This is the White
House. No, what I mean is we are *calling* the White
House. Honey," he cried, in defeat, "Can I make this
a *credit card call?*" and hunched over his card, reading out the numbers, he gave up the prestigious for-
mality of *returning* a President's call and placed the call
himself.

Aaron came in from the locker room and sat down
in Mathews's chair. He took the phone and after a
while he said, barely audibly, "Thank you very much,
Mr. President. Yeh. It was a long struggle, but I finally
made it."

Aaron leaned forward in the red leather chair, his
head down, as if the connection were bad, and he was
having trouble hearing. The President was apparently

telling him that it was a record that would stand un-challenged. Or would it?

"Well, there's Reggie Jackson over there at Oakland. And Johnny Bench. If they play long enough. That's the important thing . . . to stay healthy. This is my 21st season, and I have been fortunate enough not to sustain the long injuries."

The President was offering him an invitation to the White House.

"I'd certainly like to accept that invitation. Thank you very much."

Donald Davidson was making frantic hand motions at the end of the desk.

"Wait a minute," Aaron said. "Donald Davidson would like to say something to you."

Davidson took the phone, cupping it in his small hands, and he asked the President to give his best to David and Julie Eisenhower, hoping that all three of them had received the little clip-on 715 pin.

"Bye-bye," Davidson said cheerily, and he hung up the phone. For a second or so the two of them looked out, quite dreamily, into the middle distance, thinking back on the voice that had come to them over the wires; Aaron rocked back and forth in the red leather chair, oddly out of place in his baseball outfit, like a man who had dropped in from a fancy dress party.

He said, "It's strange to think of him watching it." He smiled. "Yeah." Then he pulled himself out of the chair and hurried out to the locker room for the ramp that led down to the dugout.

The Announcer

I found Milo Hamilton the next day in the ball park. That morning the *Atlanta Constitution* had published a transcript of Curt Gowdy describing the home run over NBC television:

And another standing ovation, five for him. He's gonna set all kinds of records tonight. Fantastic . . . you gotta feel the excitement . . . He's already broken the National League record for runs scored . . . he scored a run in the second, passing Willie Mays . . . a ball to him . . . now they boo Al Downing again . . . he's keeping that ball low and away from him. He's going to make him pull [sic] that ball . . . that's what Aaron has been doing trying to get this momentous home run. Normally he'll go to right center field with that ball . . . There's a long drive . . . the ball's hit deep . . . deep . . . and it's gone! He did it. Henry Aaron is the all-time home-run leader now."

I had looked through the paper but could not find any transcript of Hamilton's words. I thought Gowdy's were fine, if somewhat functional. Of course, on television he would be letting the picture speak for the event.

"Well, what was it?" I asked Hamilton. "You promised to tell me."

We sat in his office with its window that looked down on the diamond—what Thomas Wolfe had called "the velvet and unalterable geometry of the playing field." What a good phrase *that* was.

"It didn't work out quite the way I'd planned," Hamilton said. "First of all, the sequence of comparing Ruth and Aaron as Henry circled the bases was wiped out. I'd wanted to use the bases as touchstones in his career . . ."

"I remember," I said.

"But it was obviously going to be impossible. There wasn't time. Aaron circled the bases too quickly! He's not one to slow down and glory in his occasion. And then there was the tremendous crowd noise and the burst of fireworks above the center-field rim. Pretty hard to do much with that going on."

"What about the big sentence at the moment of impact?" I asked.

"Well, for home run number 714 I decided on 'Henry has tied the Babe!' That's what I said in Cincinnati. As for 715, the tie breaker, I came up with . . ."

"Yes?"

" 'Baseball has a new home-run king! It's Henry Aaron!' "

"Oh."

"You look disappointed."

"Well, not really," I said, admitting to myself that while the phrase was not earthshaking (or in the case of the latter, especially grammatical) anything else would have sounded hollow and forced.

"The fact is I didn't even say what I wanted to say. The tapes show that I said, 'It's 715! There's a new home-run *champion* . . .' "

"I thought it was going to be a 21-gun-salute kind of thing, *'mirabile dictu!'*—something like that."

"Say again."

What would be remembered about the instant? I asked.

Hamilton said he had been startled during his commentary by something he had never seen before in his nine years of describing the Braves in action: as Aaron turned third base, his solemn face suddenly broke into a bright grin, as surprising to see considering his usual mien as if he had started doing an Irish jig coming down the base path toward the plate. Hamilton was struck by it, but he never had time to describe it to his audience; by the time he recovered, Aaron was running into the pack of players and dignitaries with more streaming from both benches and the grandstand. "I had those things to describe to the listeners. But it's the one sight I'll particularly remember of that day . . ."

I talked to the other broadcasters afterward and was surprised that each of them, like Hamilton, had a special image of what they had seen which they had not described to their listeners, almost as if there was something of the day they wished to take away and secrete somewhere up in the attic.

For Tony Kubek, of the NBC crew, who had seen Mantle belt home-run balls out of stadiums and who batted in front of Roger Maris when he hit 61 home runs—all of that suddenly seemed obscure beside

Aaron's feat. Never had he had such an odd feeling in a ballpark—everyone there for a weird *happening,* that's what it reminded him of, with not a person there not convinced that he was going to watch Aaron perform. They settled down to see it, somewhat chilled by the wind sifting in through the gate openings. The weird aspect was heightened by what came *after*—that once Aaron had fulfilled his function, the stadium emptied, TV sets across the country were undoubtedly turned off by the millions, and even the ballplayers themselves stumbled around for the rest of the game as if in a trance. Everyone seemed to be saying, It's been done— let's shut down the shop—let's pack up and go home. The Dodgers made 6 errors, and though this was by no means a record (the Detroit Tigers made 12 errors against the Chicago American League team in 1901), Walter Alston, their manager, could not remember a game as sloppily played. Even in the broadcast booth an astonishing number of mistakes cropped up—"the sort of errors we rarely make," Kubek said. "We goofed on Aaron's records; we spent a lot of time correcting each other. We just didn't seem to care."

Curt Gowdy remembered of the instant: "Of course, I think I'll always remember the swing itself, the arc of the bat, and then seeing that the ball had enough loft to go a long way. And also the drama of *when* he did it—out goes 715 with the first swing of his bat in his home park . . . after hitting 714 with his first swing of the *season.* The superstars seem to have a knack for this sort of improbability. Everyone remembers that Ted Williams finished his career in Fenway Park with a home run on that gray day. But then the astonishing thing is that he hit a home run off Dizzy Trout the last time he came to bat before going into the service in Korea. His first time up on his return was as a pinch hitter against Mike Garcia. Damned if he didn't hit a homer off *him.* But what I'll truly remember about the night in Atlanta is the odd presentiment I felt when he spoke during the pregame ceremonies of 'getting this thing over with.' I remember thinking back to what Joe Louis said before that famous Louis-Conn fight . . . that

'he can run but he can't hide.' Aaron said his phrase
with that same sense of finality—so that the home run
seemed almost inevitable. Well, Mr. Aaron 'obliged,'
didn't he?"

The Hitter

Aaron himself does not remember very much
about that run around the bases. The tension, the long
haul, the discomfiture of the constant yammering, the
hate mail—perhaps all of that was symbolized by 715,
and to hit it produced a welcome mental block. Aaron
had always said that the most important home run in
his life was number 109, an undistinguished number,
but it was a home run hit in the 11th inning of a 2–2
tie which defeated the St. Louis Cardinals and gave the
Braves—the Milwaukee Braves, then—the 1957 pennant. Aaron has a very clear memory of his reaction as
he circled the base paths in the enormous tumult of
rejoicing. He suddenly remembered Bobby Thomson's
Miracle home run of the 1951 play-off and how he
had heard about it over somebody's radio as he was
coming home from school in Mobile, Alabama; he had
begun running as if coming down from third toward his
teammates waiting at an imaginary plate. "That had
always been my idea of the most important homer,"
Aaron said in 1957. "Now I've got one for myself. For
the first time in my life I'm excited."
But about 715 he remembered only his relief that it
was over with, and the vague happiness, that a weight
"like a stove" had been lifted from his back, and that
his legs seemed rubbery as he took the tour of the bases,
the Dodger second baseman and shortstop sticking out
their hands to congratulate him. "I don't remember the
noise," he said as he tried to recall. "Or the two kids
that ran on the field. My teammates at home plate, I
remember seeing them. I remember my mother out

there and she hugging me. That's what I'll remember more than anything about that home run when I think back on it. I don't know where she came from, but she was there . . ."

The Observer

I sat in the press box a couple of days later looking down on a night game. Aaron was not playing and the crowd was slim; management excused it: the weather was cold and the schools weren't out. The thin whistles of the ballplayers exhorting each other drifted up from the playing field, and back in the left-field corner Chief Nok-A-Homa let loose his whoop; it echoed back around the park. A couple of typewriters clicked down at the far end of the press box. I wondered how to finish my own material on Aaron. I kept thinking of what Satchel Paige had once said about him—the puzzlement of the great old pitcher as he asked, "Where did he come from? Who saw him play? Nobody knows. I pitched all those years when they could never pull the ball on me, nossir—in the valley towns and up around those hills and out on the flat fields, seeing all those hitters settin' themselves in the batter's box, and he was never there and where he was nobody knows."

I began talking to a young reporter from the CBS television affiliate in town. We wondered how the Braves would commemorate the 715th home run. Aaron's most significant home runs in the home park have been marked where they came down—number 500 by a white square in the "fan-o-gram" electric announcement board, number 600 by the appropriate numerals painted in white high on the wall down the left-field foul line, and number 700 by a seat painted red among its baby blue fellows in the left-field stands. As for 715, a plaque had been thought of for placement in the wall, or in the stands, but no one was prepared for Tommy House's catch. Some clubhouse wag had suggested that the pitcher's replica, life-size, should be set out there—if not the original article, stuffed, a gloved arm outstretched.

The reporter said there was something he'd seen which he felt might interest me—a statue of Henry Aaron made in cement by an elderly black gravestone maker down in a ramshackle part of town not a quarter of a mile away from the stadium. "It's a poor area, and the old man—his name is Bailey—sells his cement blocks for ten dollars . . . to set flat in the cemetery grass with the name and the date . . . what in marble would cost a hundred dollars. On his off-time he works on this cement statuary. The statue of Aaron weighs about 2,500 pounds . . . gigantic thing."

"Do you think it belongs out there?" I asked, nodding toward the left-center-field fence where the spoke-wheeled cannon "A Yankee Carol" was set back on the enclosure grass.

"It probably belongs where it is," he said. "You'll see why."

On the way to the airport the next morning I went to the address he had given me; the taxi turned slowly up the street which ended in a dead end against a high embankment of the Speedway, the traffic roaring by above unseen. I saw the statue immediately. It stood amidst a clutter of cement forms—life-size, brightly painted in the appropriate blue, white, with red piping, and it showed Aaron at the completion of the swing of a massive brown bat, his eyes, somewhat slanted in oriental style, watching the ball sail off on its flight. Some children came down the street, and leaned up against the chicken-wire fence to look at it.

I stepped onto a porch and rang the bell. The house was one-storied, and weather-beaten, with the windows blocked by the heavy leaves of the potted plants within. Mrs. Bailey came to the screen door. She said her husband was off tending to business. I said I was sorry. I'd heard about his statue of Aaron.

She showed me around the front yard. He worked in Portland cement, she told me, and he'd been working

on the Aaron statue off and on since last spring. Just
the day before the game he and three helpers had
moved the statue out of the work shed where he'd
painted it and into the yard. Terrible amount of labor,
and she called to him a couple of times from the porch
not to strain himself. In place, it looked over the other
pieces of statuary in the yard—massive winged birds
with curved necks, a pair of girls bent like mangrove
roots in a wild dance, a memorial to John F. Kennedy
with Air Force One flying above the White House.
A number of neighbors heard about the Aaron statue
and came up the street to pass judgment before going
home to get ready to listen to the game.

Beyond Aaron's statue in a pen in the back of the
yard a police dog kept barking, pacing the wire fence;
in the middle of the pen a large bald doll hung from
a rope suspended from a tree; it spun as the dog's
shoulder brushed it and the big ruined eyes stared
like a beacon, first revolving in one direction, and
then, as the rope unwound, in the other. The dog
barked. "Linda," said Mrs. Bailey, "that's Linda."

I spoke to Mr. Bailey that evening from New York.
I said I was sorry that I'd missed seeing him and that
I had admired his impressive statue. I asked him if
he had gone to the game. He said that he had been
somewhat exhausted by his efforts that afternoon
moving the statue into place. He had relaxed in his
springback chair for the broadcast. His wife sat across
the room. When Aaron hit number 715 the two could
hear the shouts rising along the street from the neighbors' houses.

"Just then," Mr. Bailey was saying, "I kind of
thought back, and when I realized how far he had
come, and what the hardships were, and what it means
when one of us makes good, well, I shed a little tear
over that, sitting there in my chair. My wife never
knew. Oh my no! I never let on. She never saw."

Babe Ruth's 714 Home Runs

No.	Date	Opponent	Pitcher
		1915 (4)	
1	May 6	at NY	Warhop
2	Jun 2	at NY	Warhop
3	Jun 25	NY	Caldwell
4	Jul 21	at StL	James
		1916 (3)	
5	Jun 9	at Det	Dubuc
6	Jun 12	at StL	Park
7	Jun 13	at StL	Davenport
		1917 (2)	
8	Aug 10	Det	James
9	Sep 15	at NY	Munroe
		1918 (11)	
10	May 4	at NY	Russell
11	May 6	at NY	Mogridge
12	May 7	at Wash	Johnson
13	Jun 2	at Det	Erickson
14	Jun 3	at Det	Dauss
15	Jun 4	at Det	James
16	Jun 5	at Cle	Enzmann
17	Jun 15	at StL	Rogers

No.	Date	Opponent	Pitcher
18	Jun 25	at NY	Russell
19	Jun 28	at Was	Harper
20	Jun 30	at Was	Johnson

1919 (29)

No.	Date	Opponent	Pitcher
21	Apr 23	at NY	Mogridge
22	May 20	at StL	Davenport
23	May 30	at Pha	Perry
24	Jun 7	Det	Dauss
25	Jun 17	Cle	Morton
26	Jun 24	Was	Robertson
27	Jun 30	at NY	Shawkey
28	Jul 5	Pha	Johnson
29	Jul 5	Pha	Johnson
30	Jul 10	at StL	Shocker
31	Jul 12	at Chi	Danforth
32	Jul 18	at Cle	Jasper
33	Jul 18	at Cle	Coumbe
34	Jul 21	at Det	Ehmke
35	Jul 24	NY	Shawkey
36	Jul 29	Det	Leonard
37	Aug 14	at Chi	Kerr
38	Aug 16	at Chi	Mayer
39	Aug 17	at StL	Shocker
40	Aug 23	at Det	Dauss
41	Aug 24	at Det	Ayres
42	Aug 24	at Det	Love
43	Aug 25	at Det	Leonard
44	Sep 1	Was	Shaw
45	Sep 5	at Pha	Noyes
46	Sep 8	at NY	Thormahlen
47	Sep 20	Chi	Williams
48	Sep 24	at NY	Shawkey
49	Sep 27	at Was	Jordan

1920 (54)

No.	Date	Opponent	Pitcher
50	May 1	Bos	Pennock
51	May 2	Bos	Jones
52	May 11	Chi	Wilkinson
53	May 11	Chi	Kerr
54	May 12	Chi	Williams
55	May 23	StL	Weilman
56	May 25	Det	Leonard

No.	Date	Opponent	Pitcher
57	May 26	Det	Dauss
58	May 27	at Bos	Harper
59	May 27	at Bos	Kar
60	May 29	at Bos	Bush
61	May 31	Was	Johnson
62	Jun 2	Was	Zachary
63	Jun 2	Was	Carlson
64	Jun 2	Was	Snyder
65	Jun 10	at Det	Okrie
66	Jun 13	at Cle	Myers
67	Jun 16	at Chi	Faber
68	Jun 17	at Chi	Williams
69	Jun 23	at StL	Shocker
70	Jun 25	Bos	Pennock
71	Jun 25	Bos	Pennock
72	Jun 30	at Pha	Bigbee
73	Jun 30	at Pha	Perry
74	Jul 9	Det	Oldham
75	Jul 10	Det	Dauss
76	Jul 11	Det	Ehmke
77	Jul 14	StL	Davis
78	Jul 15	StL	Burwell
79	Jul 19	Chi	Kerr
80	Jul 19	Chi	Kerr
81	Jul 20	Chi	Faber
82	Jul 23	Cle	Morton
83	Jul 24	Cle	Bagby
84	Jul 25	Bos	Hoyt
85	Jul 30	at StL	Vangilder
86	Jul 31	at StL	Shocker
87	Aug 2	at Chi	Williams
88	Aug 5	at Det	Ehmke
89	Aug 6	at Det	Dauss
90	Aug 6	at Det	Dauss
91	Aug 14	at Was	Shaw
92	Aug 19	Cle	Caldwell
93	Aug 26	Chi	Kerr
94	Sep 4	at Bos	Jones
95	Sep 4	at Bos	Bush
96	Sep 9	at Cle	Coveleskie
97	Sep 10	at Cle	Caldwell
98	Sep 13	at Det	Ehmke
99	Sep 24	Was	Acosta
100	Sep 24	Was	Shaw
101	Sep 27	at Pha	Rommel
102	Sep 27	at Pha	Rommel
103	Sep 29	at Pha	Keefe

No.	Date	Opponent	Pitcher

1921 (59)

No.	Date	Opponent	Pitcher
104	Apr 16	Pha	Harris
105	Apr 20	Bos	Russell
106	Apr 21	at Pha	Moore
107	Apr 22	at Pha	Rommel
108	Apr 25	Was	Johnson
109	May 2	at Bos	Jones
110	May 6	at Was	Erickson
111	May 7	at Was	Johnson
112	May 10	at Det	Middleton
113	May 12	at Det	Dauss
114	May 14	at Cle	Bagby
115	May 17	at Cle	Uhle
116	May 25	at StL	Shocker
117	May 29	Pha	Keefe
118	May 31	at Was	Zachary
119	Jun 3	StL	Davis
120	Jun 10	Cle	Bagby
121	Jun 11	at Det	Middleton
122	Jun 12	at Det	Sutherland
123	Jun 13	at Det	Ehmke
124	Jun 13	at Det	Ehmke
125	Jun 14	at Det	Dauss
126	Jun 14	at Det	Dauss
127	Jun 20	at Bos	Myers
128	Jun 23	at Bos	Thormahlen
129	Jun 25	Was	Johnson
130	Jun 26	Was	Mogridge
131	Jun 30	Bos	Bush
132	Jul 2	Bos	Russell
133	Jul 2	Bos	Myers
134	Jul 5	Pha	Hasty
135	Jul 11	at Chi	Kerr
136	Jul 12	at StL	Davis
137	Jul 12	at StL	Davis
138	Jul 15	at StL	Vangilder
139	Jul 18	at Det	Cole
140	Jul 30	Cle	Coveleskie
141	Jul 31	Cle	Caldwell
142	Aug 6	Det	Oldham
143	Aug 8	Chi	Wieneke
144	Aug 8	Chi	Kerr
145	Aug 10	Chi	Hodge
146	Aug 11	at Pha	Keefe
147	Aug 12	at Pha	Hasty
148	Aug 17	at Chi	Wieneke

No.	Date	Opponent	Pitcher
149	Aug 18	at Chi	Faber
150	Aug 23	at Cle	Caldwell
151	Aug 23	at Cle	Caldwell
152	Sep 2	Was	Erickson
153	Sep 3	Was	Courtney
154	Sep 5	at Bos	Karr
155	Sep 7	Bos	Pennock
156	Sep 8	at Pha	Rommel
157	Sep 9	at Pha	Naylor
158	Sep 15	StL	Bayne
159	Sep 16	StL	Shocker
160	Sep 26	Cle	Coveleskie
161	Sep 26	Cle	Uhle
162	Oct 2	Bos	Fullerton

1922 (35)

No.	Date	Opponent	Pitcher
163	May 22	StL	Vangilder
164	May 30	Pha	Heimach
165	Jun 4	Pha	Heimach
166	Jun 8	at Chi	Robertson
167	Jun 9	at Chi	Courtney
168	Jun 10	at StL	Shocker
169	Jun 19	at Cle	Mails
170	Jun 26	at Bos	Quinn
171	Jul 1	at Pha	Rommel
172	Jul 1	at Pha	Heimach
173	Jul 1	at Pha	Heimach
174	Jul 2	Pha	Yarrison
175	Jul 3	at Pha	Eckert
176	Jul 6	Cle	Mails
177	Jul 17	Chi	Robertson
178	Jul 26	at StL	Wright
179	Jul 26	at StL	Bayne
180	Jul 29	at Chi	Hodge
181	Aug 4	at Cle	Mails
182	Aug 6	at Det	Johnson
183	Aug 9	at Det	Cole
184	Aug 16	Det	Johnson
185	Aug 18	Chi	Davenport
186	Aug 19	Chi	Leverette
187	Aug 20	Chi	Faber
188	Aug 20	Chi	Faber
189	Aug 29	Was	Johnson
190	Aug 30	Was	Francis

No.	Date	Opponent	Pitcher
191	Sep 5	Bos	Pennock
192	Sep 11	at Pha	Naylor
193	Sep 11	at Pha	Schilling
194	Sep 14	at Chi	Leverette
195	Sep 17	at StL	Pruett
196	Sep 19	at Det	Pillette
197	Sep 21	at Det	Dauss

1923 (41)

No.	Date	Opponent	Pitcher
198	Apr 18	Bos	Ehmke
199	Apr 24	Was	Russell
200	May 12	at Det	Pillette
201	May 15	at Det	Collins
202	May 17	at StL	Bayne
203	May 18	at StL	Wright
204	May 19	at StL	Pruett
205	May 22	at Chi	Cvengros
206	May 26	at Pha	Hasty
207	May 30	at Was	Johnson
208	May 30	at Was	Mogridge
209	Jun 8	Chi	Cvengros
210	Jun 12	Cle	Uhle
211	Jun 17	Det	Dauss
212	Jul 2	Was	Zachary
213	Jul 3	Was	Mogridge
214	Jul 7	at StL	Vangilder
215	Jul 7	at StL	Vangilder
216	Jul 9	at StL	Davis
217	Jul 12	at Chi	Lyons
218	Jul 14	at Cle	Metevier
219	Jul 18	at Det	Holloway
220	Jul 24	at Pha	Walberg
221	Jul 27	at Pha	Naylor
222	Aug 1	Cle	Smith
223	Aug 5	StL	Kolp
224	Aug 5	StL	Kolp
225	Aug 11	Det	Dauss
226	Aug 12	Det	Johnson
227	Aug 15	at StL	Shocker
228	Aug 17	at StL	Vangilder
229	Aug 18	at Chi	Cvengros
230	Sep 5	at Pha	Hulvey
231	Sep 9	Bos	Murray
232	Sep 10	Bos	Quinn
233	Sep 13	Chi	Blankenship

No.	Date	Opponent	Pitcher
234	Sep 16	Cle	Uhle
235	Sep 28	at Bos	Ehmke
236	Oct 4	Pha	Hasty
237	Oct 5	Pha	Walberg
238	Oct 7	Pha	Harris

1924 (46)

No.	Date	Opponent	Pitcher
239	Apr 20	at Was	Johnson
240	Apr 23	Bos	Howe
241	Apr 25	Bos	Piercy
242	Apr 28	at Pha	Harris
243	Apr 28	at Pha	Baumgartner
244	May 5	Pha	Hasty
245	May 10	Chi	Thurston
246	May 13	Chi	Lyons
247	May 15	StL	Wingard
248	May 23	Det	Cole
249	May 26	Det	Stoner
250	May 30	Pha	Harris
251	May 31	Pha	Gray
252	Jun 6	at Chi	McWeeney
253	Jun 12	at Det	Johnson
254	Jun 17	at Cle	Uhle
255	Jun 21	Bos	Quinn
256	Jun 25	Was	Marberry
257	Jun 30	at Pha	Meeker
258	Jul 1	at Pha	Burns
259	Jul 3	at Pha	Gray
260	Jul 6	at Was	Martina
261	Jul 10	Chi	Connally
262	Jul 11	Chi	Mangum
263	Jul 14	StL	Wingard
264	Jul 14	StL	Wingard
265	Jul 19	Cle	Coveleskie
266	Jul 20	Cle	Metevier
267	Jul 23	Det	Dauss
268	Jul 26	Chi	Connally
269	Jul 28	Chi	Cvengros
270	Jul 29	at Chi	Thurston
271	Jul 31	at StL	Danforth
272	Aug 4	at Det	Collins
273	Aug 5	at Det	Stoner
274	Aug 6	at Det	Whitehill
275	Aug 8	at Cle	Metevier
276	Aug 8	at Cle	Messenger

No.	Date	Opponent	Pitcher
277	Aug 24	Det	Leonard
278	Aug 25	Cle	Uhle
279	Aug 28	Was	Zachery
280	Aug 28	Was	Russell
281	Sep 6	Pha	Meeker
282	Sep 8	at Bos	Fullerton
283	Sep 11	at Bos	Ehmke
284	Sep 13	at Chi	Lyons

1925 (25)

285	Jun 11	Cle	Miller
286	Jun 14	Det	Leonard
287	Jun 16	Det	Whitehill
288	Jul 1	at Bos	Fuhr
289	Jul 1	at Bos	Ross
290	Jul 2	at Pha	Rommel
291	Jul 8	at StL	Davis
292	Jul 11	at Chi	Cvengros
293	Jul 18	at Det	Stoner
294	Jul 20	at Det	Collins
295	Jul 28	StL	Wingard
296	Aug 18	at Det	Stoner
297	Aug 22	at Cle	Uhle
298	Aug 23	at Cle	Karr
299	Aug 24	at Cle	Miller
300	Sep 8	at Bos	Ross
301	Sep 10	at Pha	Gray
302	Sep 10	at Pha	Rommel
303	Sep 12	at Pha	Walberg
304	Sep 18	StL	Giard
305	Sep 24	Chi	Connally
306	Sep 27	Det	Whitehill
307	Sep 28	Det	Holloway
308	Sep 28	Det	Dauss
309	Oct 3	Pha	Willis

1926 (47)

310	Apr 20	at Was	Johnson
311	Apr 23	Bos	Ruffing
312	Apr 24	Bos	Lundgren
313	Apr 30	Was	Coveleskie
314	May 5	at Pha	Gray
315	May 7	Det	Holloway
316	May 8	Det	Whitehill
317	May 10	Det	Gibson

No.	Date	Opponent	Pitcher
318	May 13	Cle	Shaute
319	May 13	Cle	Karr
320	May 14	Cle	Levsen
321	May 15	Chi	Thomas
322	May 19	StL	Zachary
323	May 19	StL	Ballou
324	May 20	Bos	Gaston
325	May 25	at Bos	Zahniser
326	Jun 3	Bos	Wiltse
327	Jun 3	Bos	Wiltse
328	Jun 5	at Cle	Buckeye
329	Jun 8	at Det	Stoner
330	Jun 8	at Det	Holloway
331	Jun 14	at StL	Robertson
332	Jun 22	at Was	Palmero
333	Jun 25	at Bos	Russell
334	Jun 27	at Bos	Heimach
335	Jun 29	at Pha	Gray
336	Jul 9	Cle	Smith
337	Jul 20	StL	Ballou
338	Jul 21	Chi	Blankenship
339	Jul 25	Chi	Blankenship
340	Jul 27	at StL	Zachary
341	Jul 30	at StL	Ballou
342	Jul 31	at Chi	Edwards
343	Aug 5	at Cle	Smith
344	Aug 6	at Cle	Levsen
345	Aug 9	at Det	Johns
346	Aug 11	at Was	Crowder
347	Aug 14	Was	Ruether
348	Aug 15	Bos	Wingfield
349	Aug 28	Det	Stoner
350	Sep 3	at Pha	Grove
351	Sep 11	at Det	Stoner
352	Sep 19	at Cle	Levsen
353	Sep 21	at Chi	Lyons
354	Sep 25	at StL	Vangilder
355	Sep 25	at StL	Ballou
356	Sep 25	at StL	Giard

1927 (60)

No.	Date	Opponent	Pitcher
357	Apr 15	Pha	Ehmke
358	Apr 23	at Pha	Walberg
359	Apr 24	at Was	Thurston
360	Apr 29	at Bos	Harriss
361	May 1	Pha	Quinn

No.	Date	Opponent	Pitcher
362	May 1	Pha	Walberg
363	May 10	at StL	Gaston
364	May 11	at StL	Nevers
365	May 17	at Det	Collins
366	May 22	at Cle	Karr
367	May 23	at Was	Thurston
368	May 28	Was	Thurston
369	May 29	Bos	MacFayden
370	May 30	at Pha	Walberg
371	May 31	at Pha	Quinn
372	May 31	at Pha	Ehmke
373	Jun 5	Det	Whitehill
374	Jun 7	Chi	Thomas
375	Jun 11	Cle	Buckeye
376	Jun 11	Cle	Buckeye
377	Jun 12	Cle	Uhle
378	Jun 16	StL	Zachary
379	Jun 22	at Bos	Wiltse
380	Jun 22	at Bos	Wiltse
381	Jun 30	Bos	Harriss
382	Jul 3	at Was	Lisenbee
383	Jul 8	at Det	Whitehill
384	Jul 9	at Det	Holloway
385	Jul 9	at Det	Holloway
386	Jul 12	at Cle	Shaute
387	Jul 24	at Chi	Thomas
388	Jul 26	StL	Gaston
389	Jul 26	StL	Gaston
390	Jul 28	StL	Stewart
391	Aug 5	Det	Smith
392	Aug 10	at Was	Zachary
393	Aug 16	at Chi	Thomas
394	Aug 17	at Chi	Connally
395	Aug 20	at Cle	Miller
396	Aug 22	at Cle	Shaute
397	Aug 27	at StL	Nevers
398	Aug 28	at StL	Wingard
399	Aug 31	Bos	Weizer
400	Sep 2	at Pha	Walberg
401	Sep 6	at Bos	Weizer
402	Sep 6	at Bos	Weizer
403	Sep 6	at Bos	Russell
404	Sep 7	at Bos	MacFayden
405	Sep 7	at Bos	Harriss
406	Sep 11	StL	Gaston
407	Sep 13	Cle	Hudlin
408	Sep 13	Cle	Shaute

No.	Date	Opponent	Pitcher
409	Sep 16	Chi	Blankenship
410	Sep 18	Chi	Lyons
411	Sep 21	Det	Gibson
412	Sep 22	Det	Holloway
413	Sep 27	Pha	Grove
414	Sep 29	Was	Lisenbee
415	Sep 29	Was	Hopkins
416	Sep 30	Was	Zachary

1928 (54)

No.	Date	Opponent	Pitcher
417	Apr 19	at Bos	Wiltse
418	Apr 24	Was	Lisenbee
419	Apr 24	Was	Lisenbee
420	Apr 29	at Was	Lisenbee
421	May 1	at Was	Marberry
422	May 4	Chi	Cox
423	May 10	Cle	Hudlin
424	May 12	Det	Stoner
425	May 14	Det	Vangilder
426	May 15	Det	Whitehill
427	May 15	Det	Smith
428	May 17	StL	Wiltse
429	May 22	Bos	Harriss
430	May 24	at Pha	Orwoll
431	May 25	at Pha	Walberg
432	May 25	at Pha	Rommel
433	May 29	Was	Brown
434	May 29	Was	Brown
435	May 31	Was	Hadley
436	Jun 7	at Cle	Shaute
437	Jun 10	at Chi	Faber
438	Jun 10	at Chi	Lyons
439	Jun 12	at Chi	Adkins
440	Jun 15	at StL	Crowder
441	Jun 17	at StL	Ogden
442	Jun 23	Bos	Settlemire
443	Jun 23	Bos	MacFayden
444	Jun 24	Bos	Russell
445	Jun 28	at Pha	Walberg
446	Jun 28	at Pha	Earnshaw
447	Jul 2	at Was	Braxton
448	Jul 8	StL	Blaeholder
449	Jul 11	Det	Gibson
450	Jul 15	Cle	Grant
451	Jul 16	Cle	Bayne
452	Jul 18	Chi	Lyons

No.	Date	Opponent	Pitcher
453	Jul 19	Chi	Thomas
454	Jul 19	Chi	Thomas
455	Jul 21	Chi	Walsh
456	Jul 23	at Bos	MacFayden
457	Jul 30	at Cle	Miller
458	Aug 1	at StL	Crowder
459	Aug 4	at Chi	Adkins
460	Aug 14	Chi	Adkins
461	Aug 15	Chi	Faber
462	Aug 25	Det	Smith
463	Aug 30	at Was	Jones
464	Sep 8	Was	Braxton
465	Sep 11	Pha	Grove
466	Sep 15	at StL	Crowder
467	Sep 27	at Det	Carroll
468	Sep 27	at Det	Sorrell
469	Sep 28	at Det	Page
470	Sep 30	at Det	Sorrell

1929 (46)

No.	Date	Opponent	Pitcher
471	Apr 18	Bos	Ruffing
472	Apr 28	at Was	Burke
473	May 4	at Chi	McKain
474	May 5	at Chi	Adkins
475	May 7	at StL	Crowder
476	May 10	at Det	Sorrell
477	May 19	Bos	Russell
478	May 23	at Bos	Gaston
479	May 26	at Bos	Durham
480	Jun 1	Chi	Adkins
481	Jun 21	Pha	Shores
482	Jun 21	Pha	Shores
483	Jun 26	at Was	Marberry
484	Jun 29	at Pha	Grove
485	Jun 29	at Pha	Grove
486	Jun 30	at Bos	MacFayden
487	Jul 3	Bos	Ruffing
488	Jul 9	at StL	Stewart
489	Jul 13	at Chi	McKain
490	Jul 15	at Det	Carroll
491	Jul 16	at Det	Sorrell
492	Jul 17	at Det	Whitehill
493	Jul 27	StL	Blaeholder
494	Jul 28	StL	Collins
495	Aug 1	Chi	Lyons
496	Aug 6	Was	Burke

No.	Date	Opponent	Pitcher
497	Aug 6	Was	Burke
498	Aug 7	at Pha	Ehmke
499	Aug 10	at Cle	Shoffner
500	Aug 11	at Cle	Hudlin
501	Aug 12	at Cle	Shaute
502	Aug 16	at Det	Uhle
503	Aug 17	at Det	Sorrell
504	Aug 25	at StL	Stewart
505	Aug 25	at StL	Stewart
506	Aug 28	Pha	Walberg
507	Aug 29	Was	Marberry
508	Aug 31	Was	Burke
509	Aug 31	Was	Savidge
510	Sep 1	at Bos	Bayne
511	Sep 7	Det	Carroll
512	Sep 8	Det	Sorrell
513	Sep 10	Det	Whitehill
514	Sep 10	Det	Yde
515	Sep 18	Cle	Miller
516	Sep 18	Cle	Shoffner

1930 (49)

No.	Date	Opponent	Pitcher
517	Apr 25	Bos	Gaston
518	Apr 27	Bos	Russell
519	May 4	Chi	Walsh
520	May 7	Cle	Miller
521	May 11	Det	Sorrell
522	May 18	at Bos	Morris
523	May 21	at Pha	Earnshaw
524	May 21	at Pha	Earnshaw
525	May 21	at Pha	Grove
526	May 22	at Pha	Ehmke
527	May 22	at Pha	Rommel
528	May 22	at Pha	Quinn
529	May 22	Pha	Quinn
530	May 24	Pha	Walberg
531	May 30	Bos	Lisenbee
532	Jun 1	Bos	Gaston
533	Jun 3	at Chi	Lyons
534	Jun 4	at Chi	Caraway
535	Jun 7	at StL	Stewart
536	Jun 12	at Det	Sullivan
537	Jun 15	at Cle	Bean
538	Jun 19	Det	Uhle
539	Jun 21	Det	Hogsett

No.	Date	Opponent	Pitcher
540	Jun 23	StL	Kimsey
541	Jun 25	StL	Blaeholder
542	Jun 25	StL	Holshauser
543	Jun 27	Cle	Miller
544	Jun 28	Cle	Holloway
545	Jun 28	Cle	Gliatto
546	Jun 30	Chi	Thomas
547	Jul 2	Chi	Henry
548	Jul 4	at Was	Marberry
549	Jul 18	at StL	Gray
550	Jul 20	at Cle	Shoffner
551	Jul 21	at Cle	Miller
552	Jul 24	at Det	Cantrell
553	Aug 1	at Bos	Lisenbee
554	Aug 1	at Bos	Gaston
555	Aug 2	Was	Marberry
556	Aug 3	Pha	Walberg
557	Aug 5	Was	Hadley
558	Aug 10	StL	Coffman
559	Aug 12	Det	Hoyt
560	Aug 17	Chi	Henry
561	Sep 5	Was	Crowder
562	Sep 12	at Det	Wyatt
563	Sep 20	at Chi	Thomas
564	Sep 27	at Pha	Earnshaw
565	Sep 27	at Pha	Earnshaw

1931 (46)

No.	Date	Opponent	Pitcher
566	Apr 14	Bos	Durham
567	Apr 20	Pha	Earnshaw
568	Apr 20	Pha	Earnshaw
569	May 3	Was	Fischer
570	May 21	at Cle	Hudlin
571	May 24	Pha	Walberg
572	May 26	at Pha	McDonald
573	May 28	at Pha	Walberg
574	May 31	at Was	Brown
575	Jun 5	StL	Gray
576	Jun 6	Cle	Miller
577	Jun 19	at StL	Stiles
578	Jun 21	at StL	Stewart
579	Jun 23	at Chi	McKain
580	Jun 24	at Chi	Braxton
581	Jun 25	at Chi	Thomas

No.	Date	Opponent	Pitcher
582	Jun 28	at Cle	Hudlin
583	Jun 29	at Cle	Shoffner
584	Jul 2	at Det	Hoyt
585	Jul 4	Was	Fischer
586	Jul 8	Bos	Russell
587	Jul 16	Cle	Brown
588	Jul 17	Cle	Ferrell
589	Jul 22	Det	Bridges
590	Jul 22	Det	Sullivan
591	Jul 23	Det	Whitehill
592	Jul 27	Chi	Frazier
593	Jul 29	Chi	Faber
594	Aug 5	at Bos	Lisenbee
595	Aug 6	Pha	Walberg
596	Aug 13	at Cle	Harder
597	Aug 15	at Det	Uhle
598	Aug 16	at Det	Herring
599	Aug 20	at StL	Herbert
600	Aug 21	at StL	Blaeholder
601	Aug 23	at Chi	Bowler
602	Aug 24	at Chi	Thomas
603	Sep 2	Bos	Lisenbee
604	Sep 7	at Pha	Hoyt
605	Sep 7	at Pha	Hoyt
606	Sep 17	StL	Gray
607	Sep 17	StL	Gray
608	Sep 18	StL	Stewart
609	Sep 20	Cle	Connally
610	Sep 25	Was	Crowder
611	Sep 25	Was	Crowder

1932 (41)

No.	Date	Opponent	Pitcher
612	Apr 12	at Pha	Earnshaw
613	Apr 12	at Pha	Earnshaw
614	Apr 16	at Bos	Weiland
615	Apr 20	Pha	Grove
616	Apr 23	Pha	Walberg
617	Apr 30	Bos	Lisenbee
618	May 18	Cle	Brown
619	May 19	Was	Fischer
620	May 21	Was	Brown
621	May 21	Was	Ragland
622	May 24	Pha	Walberg
623	May 28	at Was	Brown

No.	Date	Opponent	Pitcher
624	May 28	at Was	Weaver
625	May 29	at Was	Ragland
626	Jun 3	at Pha	Earnshaw
627	Jun 5	Bos	Weiland
628	Jun 8	at Det	Whitehill
629	Jun 11	at Cle	Ferrell
630	Jun 12	at Cle	Harder
631	Jun 12	at Cle	Pearson
632	Jun 13	at Cle	Russell
633	Jun 23	at StL	Herbert
634	Jul 4	at Was	Brown
635	Jul 9	Det	Whitehill
636	Jul 13	StL	Herbert
637	Jul 14	Cle	Brown
638	Jul 28	at Cle	Ferrell
639	Jul 28	at Cle	Connally
640	Jul 29	at Cle	Brown
641	Jul 31	at Det	Uhle
642	Aug 7	at StL	Stewart
643	Aug 9	at StL	Cooney
644	Aug 14	at Was	Weaver
645	Aug 17	Det	Sorrell
646	Aug 19	Det	Bridges
647	Aug 25	Cle	Hildebrand
648	Aug 26	Cle	Ferrell
649	Aug 28	Chi	Lyons
650	Aug 28	Chi	Gaston
651	Sep 5	Pha	Rommel
652	Sep 24	at Bos	Michaels

1933 (34)

No.	Date	Opponent	Pitcher
653	Apr 15	Pha	Cain
654	Apr 21	at Bos	Welch
655	Apr 27	at Pha	Cain
656	Apr 28	Was	Stewart
657	Apr 30	Bos	Weiland
658	May 23	Cle	Hildebrand
659	May 28	Chi	Jones
660	May 28	Chi	Gaston
661	May 28	Chi	Faber
662	Jun 3	Pha	Freitas
663	Jun 6	Bos	Weiland
664	Jun 8	at Pha	Coombs
665	Jun 10	at Pha	Grove

128

No.	Date	Opponent	Pitcher
666	Jun 10	at Pha	Grove
667	Jun 20	at Chi	Jones
668	Jun 23	at StL	Coffman
669	Jun 28	at Det	Frazier
670	Jul 4	Was	Stewart
671	Jul 7	Det	Frazier
672	Jul 9	Det	Rowe
673	Jul 9	Det	Rowe
674	Jul 9	Det	Bridges
675	Jul 15	Chi	Gaston
676	Jul 15	Chi	Wyatt
677	Jul 29	at Was	Crowder
678	Aug 7	Was	Stewart
679	Aug 17	at StL	Blaeholder
680	Aug 19	at Chi	Kimsey
681	Sep 17	Cle	Pearson
682	Sep 17	Cle	Harder
683	Sep 23	at Bos	Welch
684	Sep 28	Was	Stewart
685	Sep 30	Was	Thomas
686	Oct 1	Bos	Kline

1934 (22)

No.	Date	Opponent	Pitcher
687	Apr 18	at Pha	McKeithan
688	Apr 21	at Bos	Weiland
689	Apr 29	Bos	Weiland
690	May 4	Det	Bridges
691	May 5	Det	Auker
692	May 5	Det	Rowe
693	May 9	StL	Weaver
694	May 28	at StL	Knott
695	Jun 3	at Pha	Cain
696	Jun 14	StL	Andrews
697	Jun 24	Chi	Jones
698	Jun 27	Chi	Gaston
699	Jul 8	Was	Weaver
700	Jul 14	at Det	Bridges
701	Jul 14	at Det	Auker
702	Jul 22	at Chi	Lyons
703	Jul 31	Bos	Ostermueller
704	Aug 4	Pha	Dietrich
705	Aug 11	at Bos	Ostermueller
706	Sep 1	Was	Stewart
707	Sep 3	Pha	Dietrich
708	Sep 29	at Was	Cohen

No.	Date	Opponent	Pitcher
		1935 (6)	
709	Apr 16	NY	Hubbell
710	Apr 21	Bkn	Benge
711	May 21	at Chi	Carleton
712	May 25	at Pit	Lucas
713	May 25	at Pit	Bush
714	May 25	at Pit	Bush

Hank Aaron's
Home Run Record

HERE IS HOW AARON STANDS IN THE MAJOR LIFETIME HITTING CATEGORIES

Leaders in Games—Cobb 3,033; Musial 3,026; Mays 3,014; AARON 2,965

At Bats—Cobb 11,429; AARON 11,291; Musial 10,972

Runs—Cobb 2,244; Ruth 2,174; Mays 2,062; AARON 2,062

Hits—Cobb 4,191; Musial 3,630; Speaker 3,515; AARON 3,509; Wagner 3,430

Total Bases—AARON 6,428

Home Runs—AARON 715; Ruth 714

Runs Batted In—Ruth 2,209; AARON 2,136

Extra Base Hits—AARON 1,394; Musial 1,377; Ruth 1,356

Doubles—Speaker 793; Musial 725; Cobb 724; Wagner 651; Lajoie 650; Waner 603; AARON 584; Gehringer 574

Two or More Homers in One Game (times accomplished)—Ruth 72; Mays 63; AARON 61

No.	Date	Inn	On Base	Opp	Pitcher
		1954 (13)			
1	Apr 23	4	0	at StL	Raschi
2	Apr 25	5	0	at StL	S. Miller
3	May 21	8	1	at Chi	Jeffcoat
4	May 22 (2nd G)	1	1	at Chi	Hacker
5	May 25	5	1	at Chi	Wehmeier
6	Jun 15	1	0	at Bkn	R. Meyer
7	Jun 17	1	0	at Bkn	Podres
8	Jun 22	4	0	at NY	Antonelli

131

No.	Date	Inn	On Base	Opp	Pitcher
9	Jun 26	4	0	at Pha	Roberts
10	Jul 2	7	1	Cin	Valentine
11	Jul 8	3	1	at Chi	Hacker
12	Jul 29	10	0	at Pit	Hetk
13	Aug 10	1	1	at StL	Raschi

1955 (27)

No.	Date	Inn	On Base	Opp	Pitcher
14	Apr 17	7	0	at Cin	Staley
15	Apr 27	8	0	at NY	Wilhelm
16	Apr 30	9	0	at Pha	Kipper
17	May 7	9	0	at StL	Moford
18	May 8	2	0	at StL	Haddix
19	May 10	8	2	Pit	Surkont
20	May 12	2	0	Bkn	Erskine
21	May 19	2	0	NY	Hearn
22	May 28	6	0	at Chi	Hacker
23	Jun 7	2	1	at NY	Antonelli
24	Jun 17	4	0	NY	Antonelli
25	Jun 24	3	2	Bkn	Erskine
26	Jun 28	6	0	Chi	S. Jones
27	Jun 29	4	1	Chi	Andre
28	Jun 29	6	0	Chi	Andre
29	Jul 2	7	1	at Cin	Collum
30	Jul 8 (2nd G)	1	1	Cin	Minarcin
31	Jul 14	6	0	at Pha	R. Miller
32	Jul 16	8	1	at NY	Maglie
33	Jul 21	4	0	at Pit	Donoso
34	Jul 22	6	0	at Bkn	Craig
35	Jul 24 (2nd G)	8	1	at Bkn	Roebuck
36	Aug 7 (1st G)	8	1	Pit	Donoso
37	Aug 9	4	0	StL	L. Jackson
38	Aug 19	3	1	Chi	Hacker
39	Sep 4	1	1	Cin	Klippstein
40	Sep 4	6	0	Cin	Black

1956 (26)

No.	Date	Inn	On Base	Opp	Pitcher
41	Apr 17	6	0	Chi	Rush
42	Apr 22 (2nd G)	3	0	at StL	L. Jackson
43	May 7	5	0	Bkn	Roebuck
44	May 22	2	0	at Bkn	Erskine
45	May 30 (1st G)	1	0	at Chi	R. Meyer
46	May 30 (2nd G)	6	0	at Chi	Hacker
47	Jun 6	1	1	Bkn	Newcombe
48	Jun 27	2	0	at Pha	Haddix
49	Jul 4 (2nd G)	8	2	StL	Wehmeier

No.	Date	Inn	On Base	Opp	Pitcher
50	Jul 6	7	0	Chi	Kaiser
51	Jul 16	4	0	Pit	Kline
52	Jul 17	7	2	NY	McCall
53	Jul 20	1	1	Pha	S. Miller
54	Jul 22 (1st G)	8	0	Pha	Flowers
55	Jul 26	1	1	at NY	Antonelli
56	Jul 30	7	1	at Bkn	Lehman
57	Aug 5	3	2	at Pit	Kline
58	Aug 19	8	1	at Cin	Acker
59	Aug 23	5	0	Pha	Simmons
60	Aug 26	3	1	Bkn	Craig
61	Sep 1	3	0	StL	Mizell
62	Sep 3 (1st G)	4	0	Cin	Klippstein
63	Sep 3 (1st G)	7	0	Cin	Klippstein
64	Sep 3 (2nd G)	8	0	Cin	Lawrence
65	Sep 13 (2nd G)	11	0	at Pha	Roberts
66	Sep 15	7	2	at Pha	R. Miller

1957 (44)

No.	Date	Inn	On Base	Opp	Pitcher
67	Apr 18	6	0	Cin	Jeffcoat
68	Apr 22	2	0	Chi	Rush
69	Apr 24	3	2	StL	Wehmeier
70	Apr 27	1	0	at Cin	Hacker
71	May 3	6	2	at Pit	Friend
72	May 5	4	2	at Bkn	Bessent
73	May 11	7	0	StL	Schmidt
74	May 12 (1st G)	4	1	at StL	Dickson
75	May 12 (2nd G)	3	1	StL	Wehmeier
76	May 18	3	0	Pit	Law
77	May 18	4	2	Pit	R. Smith
78	May 27	8	1	Cin	Klippstein
79	Jun 4	3	1	at NY	S. Miller
80	Jun 9 (1st G)	7	0	at Pit	Friend
81	Jun 9 (2nd G)	7	0	at Pit	Kline
82	Jun 12	9	0	at Bkn	Roebuck
83	Jun 14	6	2	at Pha	Cardwell
84	Jun 15	2	0	at Pha	Haddix
85	Jun 19	3	0	NY	Gomez
86	Jun 26	5	0	Bkn	Newcombe
87	Jun 29	6	2	Pit	O'Brien
88	Jun 30 (1st G)	1	0	Pit	Law
89	Jun 30 (2nd G)	4	0	Pit	Trimble
90	Jul 1	1	0	at StL	Dickson
91	Jul 3	1	1	at Cin	Jeffcoat
92	Jul 4	7	1	at Cin	Gross

No.	Date	Inn	On Base	Opp	Pitcher
93	Jul 5	9	0	Chi	Elston
94	Jul 12	6	0	at Pit	Law
95	Jul 16	1	1	at Pha	Haddix
96	Jul 25	4	0	Pha	Roberts
97	Aug 4	6	2	Bkn	Erskine
98	Aug 9	3	1	at StL	McDaniel
99	Aug 15	1	2	at Cin	Jeffcoat
100	Aug 15	7	1	at Cin	Gross
101	Aug 22	1	2	at Bkn	Maglie
102	Aug 23	4	0	at Bkn	Koufax
103	Aug 24	4	0	at Bkn	Podres
104	Aug 31	1	1	at Cin	Nuxhall
105	Sep 3	8	2	at Chi	Littlefield
106	Sep 10	4	0	Pit	Douglas
107	Sep 17	8	0	NY	Barclay
108	Sep 22	4	0	at Chi	Drott
109	Sep 23	11	1	StL	Muffett
110	Sep 24	1	3	StL	S. Jones

1958 (30)

No.	Date	Inn	On Base	Opp	Pitcher
111	Apr 20	7	0	at Pha	Roberts
112	Apr 22	4	2	at Pit	Kline
113	Apr 24	3	0	at Cin	Lawrence
114	Apr 24	5	0	at Cin	Rabe
115	May 13	4	0	at Pha	Roberts
116	May 31	1	0	at Pit	Kline
117	Jun 3	4	0	at SF	Gomez
118	Jun 3	9	0	at SF	Grissom
119	Jun 8	5	0	at LA	Podres
120	Jun 10	3	2	at Chi	Drott
121	Jun 20	8	3	StL	Muffett
122	Jun 27	4	0	LA	Koufax
123	Jun 28	7	0	LA	Erskine
124	Jun 29	6	3	LA	Drysdale
125	Jul 12	6	1	at SF	Antonelli
126	Jul 15	2	0	at StL	Maglie
127	Jul 15	4	0	at StL	Maglie
128	Jul 16	5	0	at StL	Stobbs
129	Jul 18	6	0	at Chi	Briggs
130	Jul 19	1	1	at Chi	Drabowsky
131	Jul 25 (2nd G)	7	0	Chi	Elston
132	Jul 27	1	1	Chi	Hillman
133	Jul 31	4	0	LA	Podres
134	Aug 2	7	0	SF	Monzant

134

No.	Date	Inn	On Base	Opp	Pitcher
135	Aug 6	1	1	at Pit	Law
136	Aug 19	7	1	at LA	Podres
137	Aug 21	4	0	at LA	Koufax
138	Aug 24	10	1	at SF	Worthington
139	Sep 12	3	2	StL	Mabe
140	Sep 21	7	1	at Cin	Acker

1959 (39)

No.	Date	Inn	On Base	Opp	Pitcher
141	Apr 11	3	0	at Pit	Law
142	Apr 18	7	2	Pit	Law
143	Apr 23	9	0	at Pha	Semproch
144	Apr 26	4	0	at Cin	Jeffcoat
145	Apr 29	6	0	at StL	Blaylock
146	Apr 30	4	0	at StL	Kellner
147	May 3	1	0	SF	Antonelli
148	May 3	4	0	SF	Antonelli
149	May 16	3	2	at LA	McDevitt
150	May 16	9	0	at LA	Koufax
151	May 17	5	1	at LA	Drysdale
152	May 20	6	0	at SF	McCormick
153	May 22	1	1	at Pha	Roberts
154	May 30	6	0	Pha	Cardwell
155	Jun 3	7	0	SF	Worthington
156	Jun 10	1	0	at StL	Kellner
157	Jun 21	1	1	at SF	Antonelli
158	Jun 21	6	1	at SF	S. Miller
159	Jun 21	7	1	at SF	G. Jones
160	Jun 24	1	2	at StL	Ricketts
161	Jun 25	3	1	StL	Mizell
162	Jul 3	8	1	at Pit	Witt
163	Jul 11	7	0	LA	Drysdale
164	Jul 14	6	0	at Chi	Henry
165	Jul 29	1	1	Chi	Hillman
166	Jul 29	3	0	Chi	Hillman
167	Jul 30	3	0	Chi	Ceccarelli
168	Jul 31	8	0	StL	Jeffcoat
169	Aug 1	6	0	StL	Broglio
170	Aug 12	5	0	at Cin	O'Toole
171	Aug 17 (1st G)	8	0	LA	Labine
172	Aug 18	6	0	LA	Drysdale
173	Aug 18	11	0	LA	Drysdale
174	Aug 28	4	0	at Chi	Buzhardt
175	Aug 29	4	0	at Chi	Henry
176	Aug 29	9	0	at Chi	Elston

No.	Date	Inn	On Base	Opp	Pitcher
177	Sep 2	6	1	Pha	Roberts
178	Sep 7 (1st G)	1	1	Pit	Friend
179	Sep 20	1	0	at Pha	Roberts

1960 (40)

No.	Date	Inn	On Base	Opp	Pitcher
180	Apr 14	1	1	at Pha	Simmons
181	Apr 16	6	2	at Pha	Gomez
182	Apr 22	3	0	at Pit	Friend
183	Apr 27	1	0	at Cin	Hook
184	May 5	6	0	at LA	Podres
185	May 13	4	0	Pit	Friend
186	May 15 (1st G)	7	0	Pit	Haddix
187	May 15 (2nd G)	1	2	Pit	Daniels
188	May 17	2	0	LA	Drysdale
189	Jun 2	4	0	at Pha	Gomez
190	Jun 3	3	0	Cin	Hook
191	Jun 4	5	0	Cin	Newcombe
192	Jun 12	9	0	at SF	Byerly
193	Jun 20	2	0	LA	Drysdale
194	Jun 20	6	0	LA	Drysdale
195	Jun 21 (1st G)	4	1	SF	McCormick
196	Jun 24	1	1	LA	Koufax
197	Jun 29 (2nd G)	2	0	at Chi	Anderson
198	Jul 1 (2nd G)	8	2	at StL	Simmons
199	Jul 3	4	0	at StL	Kline
200	Jul 3	7	0	at StL	Kline
201	Jul 4 (1st G)	8	1	Pit	Friend
202	Jul 7	6	0	Pha	Short
203	Jul 8	4	0	Cin	Hook
204	Jul 19	8	1	StL	Kline
205	Jul 20	4	0	StL	Broglio
206	Jul 22	8	1	at Chi	Elston
207	Jul 23	9	0	at Chi	Cardwell
208	Aug 4	9	0	at StL	Sadecki
209	Aug 5	8	0	Chi	Moorhead
210	Aug 16	4	0	at Cin	Hook
211	Aug 17	8	1	at Cin	Brosnan
212	Aug 23	6	0	at LA	Roebuck
213	Aug 30	8	2	StL	Bauta
214	Sep 8	1	0	SF	McCormick
215	Sep 9	4	1	LA	Williams
216	Sep 10	1	2	LA	Craig
217	Sep 21	6	0	Cin	O'Toole
218	Sep 30	1	1	at Pit	Law
219	Sep 30	8	1	at Pit	Olivo

No.	Date	Inn	On Base	Opp	Pitcher

1961 (34)

No.	Date	Inn	On Base	Opp	Pitcher
220	Apr 14	7	0	at Chi	Anderson
221	Apr 30	1	2	SF	Loes
222	Apr 30	6	0	SF	Loes
223	May 12	1	1	at SF	S. Jones
224	May 13	1	2	at SF	Marichal
225	May 21 (2nd G)	4	1	at Cin	Maloney
226	May 26	8	0	LA	Farrell
227	May 28	3	1	LA	Craig
228	May 31	8	0	at Pit	Gibbon
229	Jun 8	7	0	at Cin	Maloney
230	Jun 18	3	1	LA	Drysdale
231	Jun 20	6	0	SF	McCormick
232	Jun 22	3	0	SF	Marichal
233	Jun 23	4	0	Chi	Curtis
234	Jul 1	6	0	Cin	Hook
235	Jul 2 (1st G)	3	1	Cin	O'Toole
236	Jul 4	7	0	LA	Farrell
237	Jul 5	1	1	Pha	Mahaffey
238	Jul 7	1	2	Pit	Haddix
239	Jul 7	3	1	Pit	Haddix
240	Jul 21	1	1	at Pit	Friend
241	Jul 21	6	0	at Pit	Friend
242	Jul 23 (1st G)	6	0	at Pit	Haddix
243	Jul 25	4	0	Cin	Hunt
244	Jul 26	6	0	Cin	K. Johnson
245	Jul 28	2	0	StL	L. Jackson
246	Aug 2 (2nd G)	7	3	at Chi	Anderson
247	Aug 4	7	0	at SF	McCormick
248	Aug 4	9	0	at SF	McCormick
249	Aug 12	6	1	Chi	Cardwell
250	Aug 15	6	1	Pit	Gibbon
251	Aug 25 (1st G)	4	1	at Pha	Bozhardt
252	Sep 3 (2nd G)	3	0	at Chi	Ellsworth
253	Sep 25	1	0	StL	Washburn

1962 (45)

No.	Date	Inn	On Base	Opp	Pitcher
254	Apr 15	7	0	at LA	Koufax
255	Apr 18	1	0	at SF	Sanford
256	May 3	1	0	at Pha	Mahaffey
257	May 3	9	1	at Pha	Baldschun
258	May 12 (2nd G)	5	1	at NY	Moorehad
259	May 18	2	0	NY	Craig
260	May 25	1	0	at StL	Simmons
261	May 25	7	2	at StL	Washburn

137

No.	Date	Inn	On Base	Opp	Pitcher
262	May 28	9	0	at Chi	Hobbie
263	May 31	6	1	Cin	Purkey
264	Jun 12	2	0	LA	Ortega
265	Jun 14	1	1	LA	Williams
266	Jun 15	7	3	at Pit	Olivo
267	Jun 18	3	3	at NY	Hook
268	Jun 20 (2nd G)	3	1	at NY	Hunter
269	Jun 20 (2nd G)	6	0	at NY	Hunter
270	Jun 25	5	1	at LA	Moeller
271	Jun 30	1	1	Chi	Ellsworth
272	Jul 3	4	1	at StL	Gibson
273	Jul 6	4	0	at Chi	Cardwell
274	Jul 8 (1st G)	9	2	at Chi	Ellsworth
275	Jul 12	9	3	StL	McDaniel
276	Jul 17	4	1	SF	O'Dell
277	Jul 19	2	0	SF	McCormick
278	Jul 20	2	0	at Pha	Mahaffey
279	Jul 22 (1st G)	6	0	at Pha	W. Smith
280	Jul 26	2	0	NY	Anderson
281	Jul 29	4	1	at Cin	Purkey
282	Jul 29	6	1	at Cin	Purkey
283	Aug 7	3	1	Chi	Koonce
284	Aug 14	7	0	Cin	Wills
285	Aug 19	2	0	SF	O'Dell
286	Aug 19	3	1	SF	O'Dell
287	Aug 24	2	0	at Chi	Buhl
288	Aug 25	4	1	at Chi	Cardwell
289	Aug 29	3	0	at SF	O'Dell
290	Sep 7	4	0	Pha	Bennett
291	Sep 9	6	0	Pha	Bennett
292	Sep 10	7	0	at NY	R. L. Miller
293	Sep 18	3	0	LA	Podres
294	Sep 22	8	1	at Pit	Sisk
295	Sep 23	1	0	at Pit	Friend
296	Sep 23	4	2	at Pit	Friend
297	Sep 25	3	2	NY	Hook
298	Sep 26	3	2	NY	Craig

1963 (44)

No.	Date	Inn	On Base	Opp	Pitcher
299	Apr 11	7	0	NY	Rowe
300	Apr 19	8	1	at NY	Craig
301	Apr 21 (1st G)	1	0	at NY	Hook
302	Apr 22	5	0	at LA	Drysdale
303	Apr 23	9	0	at LA	Perranoski
304	Apr 26	6	1	at SF	Stanek
305	Apr 28	9	0	at SF	Larsen

138

No.	Date	Inn	On Base	Opp	Pitcher
306	May 2	5	1	at Cin	Jay
307	May 3	5	2	Chi	Buhl
308	May 7	4	0	SF	Marichal
309	May 11	6	0	at Pha	Mahaffey
310	May 18	7	3	at Chi	McDaniel
311	May 19 (1st G)	8	1	at Chi	Ellsworth
312	May 24	1	0	Pit	Friend
313	May 30	5	0	LA	Drysdale
314	May 31	6	1	Hou	K. Johnson
315	Jun 7	9	1	at Pit	Sisk
316	Jun 12	4	2	NY	Cisco
317	Jun 17	1	1	Pit	Cardwell
318	Jun 19	3	0	Pit	Francis
319	Jun 23	3	0	SF	Sanford
320	Jun 30	1	0	at LA	Willhite
321	Jul 3	6	1	at SF	Sanford
322	Jul 4	5	1	at SF	Fisher
323	Jul 11 (1st G)	3	1	at StL	Broglio
324	Jul 13	1	2	at StL	Simmons
325	Jul 19	7	0	LA	Drysdale
326	Jul 21 (1st G)	7	0	LA	Roebuck
327	Jul 28	4	1	Cin	Maloney
328	Jul 29	1	1	Cin	Tsitouris
329	Aug 2	3	2	NY	A. Jackson
330	Aug 14	7	3	LA	Drysdale
331	Aug 23	9	1	at LA	Sherry
332	Aug 26	8	1	at Hou	Brown
333	Aug 27	4	1	at Hou	Nottebart
334	Sep 2	3	0	Pha	McLish
335	Sep 6	3	0	at Pha	McLish
336	Sep 7	3	0	at Pha	Culp
337	Sep 9	7	1	at Cin	Jay
338	Sep 10	3	0	at Cin	Tsitouris
339	Sep 10	7	0	at Cin	Tsitouris
340	Sep 15	7	1	at StL	Burdette
341	Sep 25	3	1	Cin	O'Toole
342	Sep 29	1	0	Chi	Buhl

1964 (24)

No.	Date	Inn	On Base	Opp	Pitcher
343	Apr 16	3	2	at Hou	Owens
344	May 10 (1st G)	7	0	at Pit	Friend
345	May 23	8	0	StL	Taylor
346	May 24	8	0	StL	Shantz
347	May 30 (1st G)	4	1	at Chi	Buhl
348	Jun 7	5	1	Chi	Buhl
349	Jun 8	1	1	at Hou	Brown

No.	Date	Inn	On Base	Opp	Pitcher
350	Jun 14 (1st G)	9	1	at LA	Perranoski
351	Jun 22	5	0	LA	Ortega
352	Jun 27	2	1	NY	Willey
353	Jun 28 (2nd G)	5	2	NY	Lary
354	Jun 30	5	1	at StL	Craig
355	Jul 16	1	0	SF	Perry
356	Jul 26 (1st G)	1	0	at NY	A. Jackson
357	Jul 26 (2nd G)	9	2	at NY	Hunter
358	Jul 31	9	2	at Chi	McDaniel
359	Aug 1	8	0	at Chi	Burdette
360	Aug 6	6	2	at Cin	Jay
361	Aug 11	3	1	Hou	K. Johnson
362	Aug 11	6	2	Hou	Woodeshick
363	Aug 15	4	1	at SF	Duffalo
364	Aug 24	1	0	Pha	Bennett
365	Aug 30 (2nd G)	8	2	SF	Herbel
366	Sep 3	4	0	at StL	Craig

1965 (32)

No.	Date	Inn	On Base	Opp	Pitcher
367	Apr 29	8	0	StL	Taylor
368	May 2 (2nd G)	5	0	Pha	Belinsky
369	May 4	6	0	Hou	Dierker
370	May 4	8	0	Hou	Coombs
371	May 16	3	1	at Pha	Short
372	May 30	5	1	at Hou	Dierker
373	Jun 1	8	0	at Hou	Woodeshick
374	Jun 8	8	1	at Chi	Hendley
375	Jun 10	10	1	at Chi	L. Jackson
376	Jun 12	1	0	at StL	Gibson
377	Jun 19	5	1	StL	Sadecki
378	Jun 20	6	0	StL	Purkey
379	Jun 29	9	0	at NY	McGraw
380	Jul 5	8	0	Hou	Farrell
381	Jul 7	7	0	Hou	Taylor
382	Jul 8	1	0	Hou	Nottebart
383	Jul 11	7	1	at Cin	Ellis
384	Jul 19	1	0	NY	Fisher
385	Jul 20	7	2	NY	L. Miller
386	Jul 21	1	1	at LA	Osteen
387	Jul 22	1	2	at LA	R. Miller
388	Aug 4 (1st G)	1	0	LA	Drysdale
389	Aug 4 (2nd G)	7	0	LA	Osteen
390	Aug 11	3	0	StL	Washburn
391	Aug 11	5	2	StL	Washburn
392	Aug 15	1	0	at Chi	L. Jackson
393	Aug 17	5	1	at StL	Stallard

No.	Date	Inn	On Base	Opp	Pitcher
394	Aug 31 (1st G)	3	0	at Cin	Jay
395	Sep 8	6	0	Pha	Culp
396	Sep 17	1	0	SF	Marichal
397	Sep 17	3	1	SF	Marichal
398	Sep 20	6	0	Pha	Culp

1966 (44)

No.	Date	Inn	On Base	Opp	Pitcher
399	Apr 20	1	0	at Pha	Culp
400	Apr 20	9	0	at Pha	Belinsky
401	Apr 25	5	1	at SF	Priddy
402	Apr 26	3	1	at SF	Bolin
403	Apr 27	9	0	at LA	Sutton
404	Apr 28	6	0	at LA	Drysdale
405	Apr 29	9	0	Hou	Sembera
406	May 1	9	0	Hou	Cuellar
407	May 8	1	0	at Hou	Cuellar
408	May 11	1	1	Cin	Ellis
409	May 11	5	2	Cin	Ellis
410	May 17	5	0	at StL	Simmons
411	May 18	6	1	at Pit	Law
412	May 20	2	2	Chi	Faul
413	May 21	7	0	Chi	Jenkins
414	May 27	2	0	at Chi	Broglio
415	Jun 1	6	1	SF	Herbel
416	Jun 3	9	0	StL	Gibson
417	Jun 8	1	0	at NY	Fisher
418	Jun 8	3	3	at NY	Fisher
419	Jun 14	7	1	at Pha	Craig
420	Jun 18	8	1	Pit	Law
421	Jun 19	8	0	Pit	Veale
422	Jun 21	3	0	Pha	L. Jackson
423	Jul 3	8	0	at SF	Sadecki
424	Jul 9	6	0	at LA	Koufax
425	Jul 17	7	1	Cin	Nottebart
426	Jul 21	7	0	at StL	A. Jackson
427	Jul 24 (2nd G)	4	0	at Cin	Ellis
428	Jul 26	7	0	StL	A. Jackson
429	Aug 2	5	0	at Chi	Roberts
430	Aug 13 (2nd G)	9	0	Pha	Culp
431	Aug 14	2	2	Pha	Buhl
432	Aug 22	6	1	at LA	Drysdale
433	Aug 26	6	1	NY	McGraw
434	Aug 30	7	2	Chi	Holtzman
435	Sep 5 (2nd G)	5	1	at Pit	Cardwell
436	Sep 13	1	1	at Chi	Holtzman
437	Sep 13	2	0	at Chi	Holtzman

No.	Date	Inn	On Base	Opp	Pitcher
438	Sep 22	4	2	Pit	Cardwell
439	Sep 25	4	0	Pit	Sisk
440	Sep 25	8	0	Pit	McBean
441	Sep 27	4	2	SF	Sadecki
442	Oct 1 (2nd G)	8	1	at Cin	O'Toole

1967 (39)

No.	Date	Inn	On Base	Opp	Pitcher
443	Apr 19	1	0	Hou	Giusti
444	Apr 19	4	0	Hou	Giusti
445	Apr 28	6	2	Pha	Ellsworth
446	Apr 30	6	0	Pha	Buhl
447	May 5	5	2	Cin	Ellis
448	May 10 (1st G)	8	1	at Pha	Bunning
449	May 10 (2nd G)	4	1	at Pha	L. Jackson
450	May 14	6	0	at Pit	Ribant
451	May 17	6	1	NY	Seaver
452	May 21	2	1	Pit	Blass
453	May 21	8	1	Pit	Mikkelsen
454	Jun 1	1	0	at StL	Washburn
455	Jun 2	9	1	at Cin	Ellis
456	Jun 3	1	0	at Cin	McCool
457	Jun 4	5	0	at Cin	Maloney
458	Jun 12	1	2	at Pha	Ellsworth
459	Jun 14	6	2	at Pha	Green
460	Jun 22 (2nd G)	8	1	at SF	Linzy
461	Jun 27	3	3	Hou	Blasingame
462	Jun 27	8	1	Hou	Schneider
463	Jul 5	7	2	Chi	Hartenstein
464	Jul 9	8	0	at NY	Fisher
465	Jul 14	6	0	Pha	Wise
466	Jul 21	4	1	at StL	Briles
467	Jul 22	8	1	at StL	Hughes
468	Jul 27	1	1	Cin	Ellis
469	Aug 3	3	0	at Chi	Simmons
470	Aug 12 (2nd G)	8	0	Hou	Cuellar
471	Aug 13	7	1	Hou	Sembera
472	Aug 16	3	2	SF	Bolin
473	Aug 19	5	1	at LA	Osteen
474	Aug 29	1	0	Pit	Sisk
475	Aug 31	8	0	LA	Osteen
476	Sep 3	7	1	LA	Drysdale
477	Sep 4 (1st G)	1	1	Pha	Wise
478	Sep 12	3	0	NY	Fisher
479	Sep 14	4	1	NY	Frisella
480	Sep 20	5	1	Cin	Pappas
481	Sep 26	6	2	at Cin	Pappas

No.	Date	Inn	On Base	Opp	Pitcher

1968 (29)

No.	Date	Inn	On Base	Opp	Pitcher
482	Apr 15	7	1	StL	Gibson
483	Apr 17	7	0	Chi	Hands
484	Apr 19	3	1	at Cin	Tsitouris
485	Apr 21	1	0	at Cin	Pappas
486	Apr 23	1	0	at Chi	Niekro
487	Apr 28	9	1	Pha	Wise
488	May 11	1	0	LA	Osteen
489	May 11	3	2	LA	Osteen
490	May 14	5	1	at Pha	L. Jackson
491	Jun 9 (2nd G)	1	1	at Chi	Hands
492	Jun 12	3	1	StL	Briles
493	Jun 17	4	0	Cin	Maloney
494	Jun 21	8	0	at StL	Willis
495	Jun 27	1	0	Pha	Short
496	Jun 28	8	0	at LA	Kekich
497	Jul 5	3	1	Hou	Cuellar
498	Jul 7	4	0	Hou	Dierker
499	Jul 7	5	1	Hou	Dierker
500	Jul 14	3	2	SF	McCormick
501	Jul 26 (1st G)	9	2	at Pha	G. Jackson
502	Aug 6	4	0	Chi	Niekro
503	Aug 21 (2nd G)	3	1	at Chi	Nye
504	Aug 23	5	2	Pha	Wise
505	Aug 25	4	0	Pha	L. Jackson
506	Aug 28 (2nd G)	6	0	at Pha	J. Johnson
507	Aug 29	1	0	at Pha	L. Jackson
508	Sep 11	3	1	SF	Marichal
509	Sep 22	1	0	at SF	Bolin
510	Sep 29	6	1	LA	Singer

1969 (44)

No.	Date	Inn	On Base	Opp	Pitcher
511	Apr 12	4	0	Cin	Nolan
512	Apr 16	1	1	at Hou	Lemaster
513	Apr 28	3	2	Hou	Dierker
514	May 3	3	1	LA	Osteen
515	May 13	1	0	at NY	Gentry
516	May 15	3	0	at NY	Cardwell
517	May 15	7	0	at NY	Kounce
518	May 18	7	0	at Mtl	Face
519	May 22	1	1	NY	McGraw
520	May 31	1	0	at Chi	Jenkins
521	Jun 1	5	1	at Chi	Holtzman
522	Jun 2	8	0	at StL	Waslewski
523	Jun 3	6	0	at StL	Carlton

No.	Date	Inn	On Base	Opp	Pitcher
524	Jun 6	4	0	Pit	D. Ellis
525	Jun 8 (1st G)	8	0	Pit	Hartenstein
526	Jun 11	5	0	Chi	Nye
527	Jun 12	8	2	Chi	Selma
528	Jun 17	9	0	Hou	Billingham
529	Jun 25	8	0	LA	Osteen
530	Jun 27	5	1	at Hou	Lemaster
531	Jun 30	3	2	Cin	Cloninger
532	Jul 7	3	1	at LA	Foster
533	Jul 8 (1st G)	1	0	at LA	Osteen
534	Jul 15 (1st G)	5	0	at Cin	Carroll
535	Jul 24	6	1	Mtl	Radatz
536	Jul 25	7	0	Mtl	H. Reed
537	Jul 30 (1st G)	3	0	at Pha	G. Jackson
538	Jul 31 (1st G)	6	0	at Pha	Palmer
539	Aug 9	3	0	NY	Seaver
540	Aug 13 (1st G)	3	1	Pha	Boozer
541	Aug 13 (1st G)	5	0	Pha	Boozer
542	Aug 17	6	0	StL	Carlton
543	Aug 21	6	0	at Chi	Hands
544	Aug 24	6	2	at StL	Grant
545	Aug 28	14	2	at Pit	Blass
546	Aug 28	7	3	at Pit	Dal Canton
547	Aug 30	7	0	Chi	K. Johnson
548	Sep 5	3	1	at Cin	Merritt
549	Sep 7	7	0	at Cin	Ribant
550	Sep 10	4	0	SF	Bryant
551	Sep 11	4	0	SF	McCormick
552	Sep 17	12	0	at LA	Lamb
553	Sep 21	7	2	at SD	Dukes
554	Sep 26	4	0	SD	Corkins

1970 (38)

No.	Date	Inn	On Base	Opp	Pitcher
555	Apr 9	1	1	at SD	Kirby
556	Apr 10	3	3	at Hou	Griffin
557	Apr 13	1	1	SF	Reberger
558	Apr 14	3	1	SF	Reberger
559	Apr 18	4	1	LA	Sutton
560	Apr 23	5	0	at Pit	Walker
561	Apr 28	1	0	at StL	Torrez
562	Apr 30	7	0	Chi	Cosman
563	May 1	1	0	Chi	Decker
564	May 5	2	1	Pit	Moose
565	May 6	1	1	Pit	Ellis
566	May 8	6	2	StL	Gibson
567	May 9	5	1	StL	Culver

No.	Date	Inn	On Base	Opp	Pitcher
568	May 11	10	0	at Chi	Reynolds
569	May 15	8	1	at Cin	Nolan
570	May 17 (2nd G)	3	1	at Cin	Simpson
571	Jun 2	7	1	NY	Gentry
572	Jun 18	5	1	at Mtl	Renko
573	Jun 19 (2nd G)	5	1	Hou	Lemaster
574	Jun 20	4	0	Hou	Griffin
575	Jun 21	1	1	Hou	Dierker
576	Jun 21	4	1	Hou	Dierker
577	Jun 30	1	1	at Cin	McGlothin
578	Jul 3 (2nd G)	2	1	SD	Dobson
579	Jul 17	6	1	at StL	Briles
580	Jul 25	6	1	at Chi	Jenkins
581	Jul 29	3	1	StL	Torrez
582	Jul 29	7	2	StL	Linzy
583	Aug 1	1	1	Pit	DalCanton
584	Aug 1	7	1	Pit	Pena
585	Aug 2	5	2	Pit	Ellis
586	Aug 7 (1st G)	6	1	at SD	Roberts
587	Aug 9	8	0	at SD	Dobson
588	Aug 12	2	1	Mtl	Stoneman
589	Aug 26	9	1	at NY	Gentry
590	Sep 3	3	2	LA	Foster
591	Sep 5 (2nd G)	8	1	SF	Robertson
592	Oct 1	4	0	at Cin	Washburn

1971 (47)

No.	Date	Inn	On Base	Opp	Pitcher
593	Apr 7	7	0	at Cin	McGlothin
594	Apr 10	9	1	Pit	Blass
595	Apr 13	6	0	Cin	Gullett
596	Apr 14	1	1	Cin	Cloninger
597	Apr 14	4	0	Cin	Cloninger
598	Apr 20	1	1	at Pit	Moose
599	Apr 25 (1st G)	9	0	SD	Roberts
600	Apr 27	3	1	SF	Perry
601	May 1	1	1	LA	Osteen
602	May 1	8	1	LA	Mikkelson
603	May 2	8	0	LA	Brewer
604	May 8	8	2	at SF	J. Johnson
605	May 18	1	1	NY	McAndrew
606	May 21	6	0	at NY	Ryan
607	May 27	6	0	at Mtl	McAnally
608	Jun 1	1	1	Hou	Blasingame
609	Jun 6	9	0	Chi	Hands
610	Jun 8	1	1	StL	Carlton
611	Jun 13	3	0	at Hou	Wilson

No.	Date	Inn	On Base	Opp	Pitcher
612	Jun 21 (1st G)	8	1	Mtl	Raymond
613	Jun 27	7	1	Cin	Nolan
614	Jun 27	9	1	Cin	Granger
615	Jul 4	4	0	at NY	Seaver
616	Jul 10	7	0	at Pit	Blass
617	Jul 17	3	0	LA	Alexander
618	Jul 20	9	1	SD	Roberts
619	Jul 21 (1st G)	1	1	SD	Arlin
620	Jul 21 (1st G)	3	0	SD	Arlin
621	Jul 24	6	0	at LA	Osteen
622	Jul 31	8	0	at SD	Norman
623	Aug 3	7	0	at Pha	Short
624	Aug 15	6	0	Hou	Forsch
625	Aug 20	1	0	StL	Cleveland
626	Aug 21	6	1	StL	Carlton
627	Aug 21	7	2	StL	Carlton
628	Aug 23 (1st G)	6	0	Pit	Blass
629	Aug 24	4	0	Pit	Veale
630	Aug 25	1	1	Pit	Kison
631	Aug 29	1	1	at Chi	Pizarro
632	Sep 10	11	2	SF	J. Johnson
633	Sep 11	1	1	SF	Carrithers
634	Sep 14	1	2	at Cin	Gullett
635	Sep 14	5	1	at Cin	Gullett
636	Sep 15	5	0	at Hou	Billingham
637	Sep 17	8	0	at LA	Osteen
638	Sep 21	1	0	SD	Franklin
639	Sep 26	5	0	LA	Osteen

1972 (34)

No.	Date	Inn	On Base	Opp	Pitcher
640	Apr 22	3	2	Cin	Gullett
641	Apr 23	8	0	Cin	Billingham
642	Apr 25	2	1	StL	Gibson
643	Apr 26	1	0	StL	Wise
644	May 5	1	1	at StL	Gibson
645	May 6	8	0	at StL	Wise
646	May 26	4	1	SF	Marichal
647	May 28 (1st G)	6	0	SF	Bryant
648	May 31	1	0	SD	Norman
649	Jun 10	6	3	at Pha	Twitchell
650	Jun 13	10	0	NY	Frisella
651	Jun 14	4	0	NY	Matlack
652	Jun 24 (2nd G)	8	0	at LA	Brewer
653	Jun 28 (1st G)	9	1	at SD	Corkins
654	Jun 29	6	0	at SD	Caldwell
655	Jul 2	1	1	at Hou	Roberts

No.	Date	Inn	On Base	Opp	Pitcher
656	Jul 3	7	2	at Hou	York
657	Jul 9	4	0	Pit	Briles
658	Jul 11	7	2	at StL	Santorini
659	Jul 19	1	0	at Pit	Briles
660	Aug 6	4	0	at Cin	Simpson
661	Aug 6	10	0	at Cin	Gullett
662	Aug 9	1	1	Hou	Reuss
663	Aug 13	3	1	Cin	Hall
664	Aug 16	8	0	at NY	Gentry
665	Aug 29	5	0	Mtl	Moore
666	Sep 2	1	1	Pha	Brandon
667	Sep 2	7	1	Pha	Scarce
668	Sep 13	7	0	Cin	Hall
669	Sep 13	9	0	Cin	Hall
670	Sep 17	3	1	SF	Bryant
671	Sep 26	1	0	at Cin	Gullett
672	Sep 27	1	0	at Cin	Grimsley
673	Oct 3	9	2	LA	Sutton

1973 (40)

No.	Date	Inn	On Base	Opp	Pitcher
674	Apr 11		2	at SD	Troedson
675	Apr 12		0	at SD	Norman
676	Apr 15		0	at LA	Downing
677	Apr 20		1	at Cin	Gullett
678	Apr 27		0	NY	Seaver
679	May 1		1	Mtl	Moore
680	May 1		0	Mtl	Strohmayer
681	May 5		0	at Pha	Carlton
682	May 13		1	SD	Greif
683	May 13		0	SD	Norman
684	May 16		0	at Hou	Reuss
685	May 22		0	SF	Marichal
686	May 27		1	at StL	Cleveland
687	Jun 9		0	StL	Spinks
688	Jun 9		0	StL	Andrews
689	Jun 11		2	Pit	Rooker
690	Jun 15		0	Chi	Bonham
691	Jun 16		0	Chi	Reuschel
692	Jun 22		0	at SD	Jones
693	Jun 29		1	LA	Hough
694	Jul 2		1	SF	Barr
695	Jul 8		0	at NY	Stone
696	Jul 8		1	at NY	Stone
697	Jul 13		2	Pha	Stoneman
698	Jul 17		0	NY	McGraw
699	Jul 20		1	Pha	Brett

No.	Date	On Base	Opp	Pitcher
700	Jul 21	1	Pha	Brett
701	Jul 31	0	Cin	Borbon
702	Aug 16	2	at Chi	Aker
703	Aug 17	0	at Mtl	Renko
704	Aug 18	0	at Mtl	Rogers
705	Aug 22	0	StL	Cleveland
706	Aug 28	2	Chi	Pappas
707	Sep 3	0	at SD	Kirby
708	Sep 3	2	at SD	Romo
709	Sep 8	0	Cin	Billingham
710	Sep 10	1	SF	Carrithers
711	Sep 17	0	SD	Ross
712	Sep 22	1	at Hou	Roberts
713	Sep 29	1	Hou	Reuss

1974

No.	Date	On Base	Opp	Pitcher
714	Apr 4		at Cin	Billingham
715	Apr 8		LA	Downing

Aaron's Leading
Home Run Victims

Drysdale	17	Koufax	7
Osteen	13	Simmons	7
Friend	12	Washburn	7
Cardwell	10	Carlton	6
Craig	10	Ellsworth	6
Jackson, L.	10	Fisher	6
Law	9	Hacker	6
McCormick	9		
Roberts, R.	9	Jeffcoat	6
Antonelli	8	Podres	6
Haddix	8	Wise	6
Hook	8	Blass	5
Kline	8	Briles	5
Marichal	8	Culp	5
		Erskine	5
Buhl	7	Maloney	5
Dierker	7	O'Toole	5
Ellis, S.	7	Roberts, D.	5
Gibson	7	Roebuck	5
Gullett	7	Short	5

Year - By - Year

HANK'S YEAR-BY-YEAR LIFE IN THE BIG LEAGUES

Few players in any sport have ever drawn greater ac-
claim than Atlanta's Hank Aaron. The Braves' Hammer
has matched the great Babe Ruth's all-time home run
record, and virtually every big league hitting record is
in his reach. Here is a brief summary of each season
of Hank's big league career:

1954
Hank became a regular on the Braves when Bobby
Thomson broke his ankle during spring training. On
September 5th Hank also suffered a broken ankle and
missed the remainder of his rookie season.

1955
Aaron established himself as a home run slugger, con-
necting for 27 round trippers. He also led the league in
doubles with 37 and posted a .314 batting average for
the season. Hank was selected to play in the All-Star
game for the first time.

1956
Hank won his first major league batting title with a .328
average and led the league in hits (200), total bases
(340) and doubles (34).

1957
The World Champion Braves were led by the "Hammer" and he was tops in the league in home runs, hits,
total bases and runs batted in.

1958
Hank was awarded the Gold Glove as the league's top
fielding right fielder. He led the team to its second
straight pennant, batting .326 for the season with 30
home runs and 95 RBI.

150

1959

Hank won his second National League Batting Crown, posting a .355 average. He led the league in hits (223) and total bases (400).

1960

For the second straight year Hank led the league in total bases with 334. He was also the league leader in RBI (126).

1961

Hank led the league in doubles for the third time in his career (39) and led the league in total bases for the fourth time (358). He also hit .327 with 34 homers and drove in 120 runs.

1962

Although Hank did not lead the league in any one hitting category, he nonetheless was awesome in his attack on National League pitchers.

1963

Hank was named the National League "Player of the Year" and became one of only five players to hit 30 home runs and steal 30 bases in one season. He led the league in home runs, RBI, hits and total bases.

1964

This was not a banner year for the Hammer, but for the ninth consecutive year he scored more than 100 runs and batted above .300. He was selected to play in the All-Star game for the thirteenth consecutive time.

1965

Hank led the league in doubles for the fourth time in his career with 40 and posted a .318 batting average.

1966

Teammate Eddie Mathews and Hank set a Major League record for most career home runs by teammates (863). Hank led the majors with 44 homers and 127 RBI. The titles were his third and fourth, respectively.

1967

Baseball writers voted Hank the Braves' most valuable player as he led the team in home runs (39), hits (113) and total bases (344).

1968

Hank joined the select group of Home Run Kings when he hit his 500th career homer on July 14th. He became the eighth player to accomplish that feat.

1969
The Braves won the National League's Western Division Pennant and Hank was one of the main contributors. He hit 44 home runs and drove in 97 runs while posting a .300 batting average.

1970
This year marked one of the greatest triumphs in the Hammer's career when he collected his 3000th career base hit. He joined Stan Musial as the only two living members of this select group.

1971
This year proved to be the Hammer's greatest. On the night of April 27th, Hank became only the third player in the history of baseball to hit 600 career home runs. In addition to that feat he led the team in home runs with 47, RBI (118) and recorded a .327 batting average for the season.

1972
His 648th career homer tied Willie Mays for second on the all-time homer list, and Hank then took over sole possession of the number two spot. Hank also tied the all-time National League grand slam homer mark when he hit the 14th of his career. Top spots on all-time hitting lists began to fall in rapid succession.

1973
Hank set a record for career extra base hits by breaking Musial's 1,377 record to hit 1,394. He also hit 40 home runs this season, bringing his total to just one short of Ruth's record.

HANK AARON DATES OF SIGNIFICANCE

February 5, 1934
Born in Mobile, Alabama.

November 20, 1951
Signed to play for the Indianapolis Clowns by scout Ed Scott.

June 14, 1952
Signed by Braves' scout Dewey Griggs and assigned to play for the Braves' Eau Claire, Wisconsin, farm team.

March 13, 1954
Braves left fielder Bobby Thomson broke his ankle sliding into second base, opening the outfield position for young Hank Aaron.

March 14, 1954
Hank started his first game for the Braves in spring training and also hit a home run.

April 13, 1954
Hank played in his first regular season big league game, going 0 for five against pitcher Joe Nuxhall of the Reds in Cincinnati.

April 15, 1954
Hank collected his first big league hit, going two for five in the game to lead the Braves to a 7-6 victory over the Cards.

April 23, 1954
Hank hit his first big league home run and it came against Vic Raschi of the Cards in St. Louis.

September 5, 1954
Hank broke his ankle and missed the remainder of his rookie season.

August 15, 1957
Hank hit the 100th homer of his career against Don Gross of the Reds in Cincinnati.

September 23, 1957
Hank's home run off Billy Muffett of the Cards clinched the 1957 National League pennant for the Braves. He hit it in the bottom of the 11th inning with the score tied 2-2.

October 5, 1957
Hank hit his first World Series homer against the Yankees' Bob Turley. The Braves lost the game, however, 12-3.

June 21, 1959
Hank hit three homers against the Giants in one day.

July 3, 1960
Hank hit the 200th homer of his career against Ron Kline of the Cards in St. Louis.

June 8, 1961
Hank, Eddie Mathews, Joe Adcock and Frank Thomas became the first four players ever to hit homers in succession in one inning. They did it in the seventh inning in Cincinnati.

April 4, 1974
Hank hit his 714th home run, tying Babe Ruth's 39-year record.

April 8, 1974
Hank hit his 715th home run, becoming the greatest home-run hitter of all time.

ABOUT THE AUTHOR

GEORGE PLIMPTON is a graduate of Harvard University and King's College, Cambridge University. In 1953, in Paris, he became the editor of *The Paris Review,* a literary quarterly which in 1973 celebrated its twentieth anniversary, and he has since edited the four volumes of interviews with famous literary figures entitled *Writers at Work* that first appeared in the magazine. His books include *Out of My League, Paper Lion, The Bogey Man, Mad Ducks and Bears* and a juvenile entitled *The Rabbit's Umbrella.* He is also the co-author (with Jean Stein) of an oral-history volume entitled *American Journey: The Times of Robert F. Kennedy.* A special contributor to *Sports Illustrated* and an associate editor of *Harper's Magazine,* Mr. Plimpton lives in New York City with his wife, Freddy, and a small daughter, Medora Ames.

74 75 76 77 10 9 8 7 6 5 4 3 2 1